Contributions Of Buddhism for World Peace & Social Harmony

Edited by Dr. Buddha Priya Mahathero
and Dr. Bhikṣuṇī TN Gioi Huong

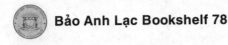

Bảo Anh Lạc Bookshelf 78

Contributions Of Buddhism
for
World Peace & Social Harmony

Buddhist Studies Seminar, Kolkata, India
July 2, 2023

Edited by
Dr. Buddha Priya Mahathero
and **Dr. Bhikṣuṇī TN Gioi Huong**

 TON GIAO Publishing

Contact:

HUONG SEN BUDDHIST TEMPLE

19865 Seaton Avenue, Perris, CA 92570, USA

Tel: 951-657-7272 Cell: 951-616-8620

Email: huongsentemple@gmail.com

Fanpage: Huong Sen

(https://www.facebook.com/Huong.Sen.Riverside)

Web: www.huongsentemple.com

First edition © Ton Giao Publishing

CONTENT

INTRODUCTION

*A*global war is brewing. Many people cannot control their greed and anger. In this atmosphere of mutual hatred, the drums of war (Ukraine–Russia, the civil war in Niger . . .) continue to ring negative for the world. With social degradation, the youth especially, have taken the path of destruction. It seems as if civilization is facing a downward spiral. It is at this time, the mindful people around the world seek spritual practice and refuge with the Lord Buddha, Dharma, and Sangha who show the tranquil pure way to balance the temper as the Buddha taught:

Anger is conquered by love
Hatred never ceases
through hatred in this world
through love alone they cease.
This is an eternal law.
This is the only way of peace.
(Dhammapada, Verse 5)

Overcome anger by love
Conquer anger by love
Conquer evil by good
Conquer the stingy by giving

Conquer the liar by truth
This is the universal way of peace.
(Dhammapada, Verse 6)

For the sake of many, Dr. Ven. Buddha Priya Mahathero (Abbot and Secretary of Siddharth United Social Welfare Mission, Chinar Park, Kolkata, India) and Dr. Ven. Bhikṣuṇī TN Gioi Huong (English Lecturer at the Vietnam Buddhist University in HCM City and Abbess of Hương Sen Buddhist Temple, California, USA) have co-organized an international seminar with the theme, **"Contributions of Buddhism for World Peace & Social Harmony,"** on July 2, 2023 at the Siddharth United Social Welfare Mission, Chinar Park, Kolkata, India.

At this Kolkata Seminar, there were twenty-three renowned speakers-spiritual peace leaders, eminent writers, and researchers presented their meaningful papers, such as Dr Siddharth M. Jondhale (Former Chancellor of Trinity World University), Professor Kishore Bhattacharjee (Viswabharati University, Shantiniketan), Professor Mahuya Mukherjee (Rabindrabharati University, Kolkata), Professor Swarnali Barua (Presidency University), Dr. Surajit Barua (Seth Anandram Jaipur College), Mr. Subhankar Barua (West Bengal Civil Service), Mr. Nima Wangdi Sherpa (Chairman and Spiritual Peace Leader, Darjeeling Chapter), Ms. Priyanka Barua (Research Scholar, Calcutta University), Mr. Saurabh Barua (Research Scholar and Engineer), Mrs. Madhumita Barua (Writer and Speaker), Mr. Pradyut Chowdhury (General Secretary, Rishra Bauddha Samity, Rishra, W.B. India), Mr. Utpal Kanti Chowdhury (President of Rishra Samaj Kalyan Samity), Dr. Palash Bandyopadyay (Eminent Writer and Physician), Ms. Shruti Barua (Writer, Sodepur-natagarh, Kolkata), and especially Dr. Ven. Buddha Priya Mahathero (the peaceful activist), Dr. Bhikṣuṇī Gioi Huong (Vietnamese-American author of eighty books), Rev. Buddharatna Bhante (Meditation Master in Bodhgaya, India), and Bhikṣuṇī TN Trí Minh (Spiritual Teacher in Canada).

Twenty-three papers from this seminar are presented from different perspectives, but carry the same idea-how to keep world peace based on the Buddha's teaching. These papers have been collected to publish as a book, *Contributions of Buddhism for World Peace & Social Harmony,* with the aim to share our Buddhist experience and knowledge and add our part to the common mission of keeping the world safe.

We would like to sincerely thank Dr. Ven. Buddha Priya Mahathero, Rev. Buddharatna Bhante, Dr. Ven. Bhikṣuṇī TN Gioi Huong, Bhikṣuṇī TN Trí Minh (younger sister of TN Gioi Huong), the Huong Sen Temple's delegate of ten monastic disciples, the Indian press media, artist singers, SUSWM staff and those who kindly supported this seminar.

Once again, thanking all the learned resource persons, speakers, delegates, and organizations who have helped us to make this international event a grand success.

May all living beings
be happy and peaceful.

Huong Sen Buddhist Temple

August 30, 2023

The Editorial Board

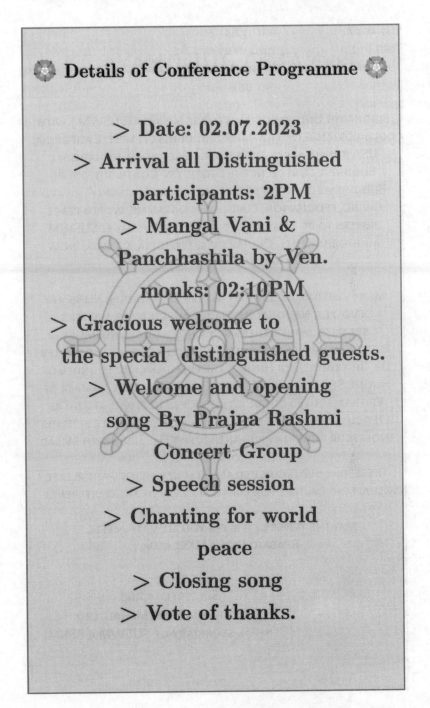

Details of Conference Programme

> Date: 02.07.2023
> Arrival all Distinguished participants: 2PM
> Mangal Vani & Panchhashila by Ven. monks: 02:10PM
> Gracious welcome to the special distinguished guests.
> Welcome and opening song By Prajna Rashmi Concert Group
> Speech session
> Chanting for world peace
> Closing song
> Vote of thanks.

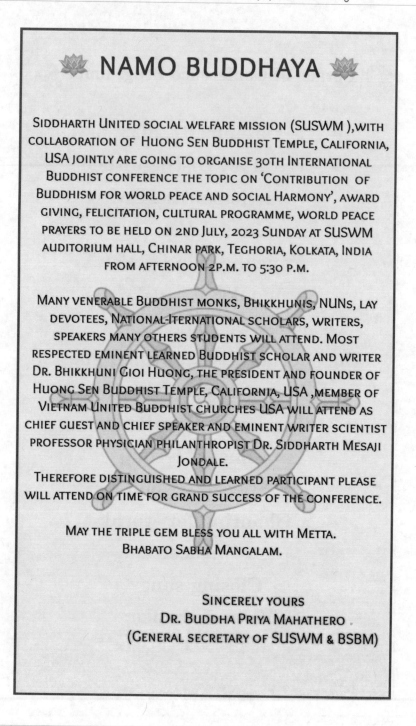

❀ NAMO BUDDHAYA ❀

SIDDHARTH UNITED SOCIAL WELFARE MISSION (SUSWM), WITH COLLABORATION OF HUONG SEN BUDDHIST TEMPLE, CALIFORNIA, USA JOINTLY ARE GOING TO ORGANISE 30TH INTERNATIONAL BUDDHIST CONFERENCE THE TOPIC ON 'CONTRIBUTION OF BUDDHISM FOR WORLD PEACE AND SOCIAL HARMONY', AWARD GIVING, FELICITATION, CULTURAL PROGRAMME, WORLD PEACE PRAYERS TO BE HELD ON 2ND JULY, 2023 SUNDAY AT SUSWM AUDITORIUM HALL, CHINAR PARK, TEGHORIA, KOLKATA, INDIA FROM AFTERNOON 2P.M. TO 5:30 P.M.

MANY VENERABLE BUDDHIST MONKS, BHIKKHUNIS, NUNS, LAY DEVOTEES, NATIONAL-ITERNATIONAL SCHOLARS, WRITERS, SPEAKERS MANY OTHERS STUDENTS WILL ATTEND. MOST RESPECTED EMINENT LEARNED BUDDHIST SCHOLAR AND WRITER DR. BHIKKHUNI GIOI HUONG, THE PRESIDENT AND FOUNDER OF HUONG SEN BUDDHIST TEMPLE, CALIFORNIA, USA, MEMBER OF VIETNAM UNITED BUDDHIST CHURCHES USA WILL ATTEND AS CHIEF GUEST AND CHIEF SPEAKER AND EMINENT WRITER SCIENTIST PROFESSOR PHYSICIAN PHILANTHROPIST DR. SIDDHARTH MESAJI JONDALE.
THEREFORE DISTINGUISHED AND LEARNED PARTICIPANT PLEASE WILL ATTEND ON TIME FOR GRAND SUCCESS OF THE CONFERENCE.

MAY THE TRIPLE GEM BLESS YOU ALL WITH METTA.
BHABATO SABHA MANGALAM.

SINCERELY YOURS
DR. BUDDHA PRIYA MAHATHERO .
(GENERAL SECRETARY OF SUSWM & BSBM)

THE GREAT CONTRIBUTION TO WORLD PEACE AND SOCIAL HARMONY OF EMPEROR ASHOKA AND EMPEROR TRẦN NHÂN TÔNG

Presented by Ven. Dr. Bhikṣuṇī TN Gioi Huong
at the Conference of Siddharth United Social Welfare Mission,
Kolkata, India

To begin with, it seems it is proper and appropriate to jot down a few sentences on the Buddha, Buddhism, and religious background of India and Vietnam before coming to the subject of concern, "The Great Contribution to World Peace and Social Harmony of Emperor Ashoka of India and Emperor Trần Nhân Tông of Vietnam."

India and Vietnam maintain centuries-old traditional relations, particularly in the field of culture along with other political, trade, and economic affiliations. Both countries equally respect and honor each other's religious and national leaders.

I. THE SAKYAMUNI BUDDHA IN INDIA

During several centuries before the Christian Era, the civilized part of India was divided into sixteen realms, eight of which were kingdoms, and the remaining were republics. Among those kingdoms the most powerful were Magadha and Kosala.

Indian map (Google)[1]

The little Sakya republic was ruled by the king of Kosala who received tribute. The Sakyas were of the Kshatriya Solar Dynasty and were called the "eslverajas" or "kings."[2] In the middle of the century, their chief was King Suddhodana who had his capital at Kapilawastu. In the year 623 BC his queen, Maha Maya, was traveling from Kapilavastu to her parent's home in Devdaha to have her first child. On her way the queen gave birth to a divine son in the Lumbini grove between two tall Sal trees.

1   https://www.buddhisttour.com/map.html
2   Bapat, P.V. 2500 Years of Buddhism. Department of Information, Government of India, New Delhi, 1959, 1–7.

An old sage named Asita visited King Suddhodana and predicted the royal baby would one day become the savior of human beings. The royal baby was named Siddhartha. The king provided all protection and gave him every comfort. When Siddhartha was young, his father, Suddhodana, arranged for him to marry a beautiful princess named Yasodhara. They had one child, a son named Rahula. Even before the marriage, Prince Siddhartha had a strong desire to leave the worldly life, which his father prevented. After the birth of his son, Siddhartha thought his son would be an obstacle to his future steps. One day he decided to leave the worldly life and accordingly, while his wife and son were sleeping, he left the palace without anyone noticing.

In his chariot he rode away passing through a forest. He discarded his royal robes, cut his long hair with his sword and became an ascetic. He went in search of teachers who could teach him the truth of life. He imbibed all that they had to teach him, but his thirst for truth remained unanswered and unquenched. He moved on and ultimately reached a picturesque land at a place presently known as Bodh Gaya. In accordance with the belief that the mind became elevated by emancipating the body, he practiced rigid austerities and resorted to different kinds of self-torture for six years. He lived in this manner and was reduced to a skeleton. At this stage he realized that physical torture was not the way to achieve enlightenment and decided to partake of food again.

Gotama Bodhisatta meditating on the Nairanjana River

After consuming a bowl of milk rice offered to him by the young girl, Sujata, daughter of a wealthy merchant, he regained good health. After several attempts to control and set the mind free, he attained enlightenment under a Bodhi tree, now known as Sri Maha Bodhi. With this, a human being was able to "experience and understand how to escape from suffering and teach others."[3] In the history of Indian religions, Buddhism occupies a unique place, firstly for throwing its portals open not only to Indians, but to all sections of the world society. From the beginning, Buddhism has always been based on "peace, tolerance, nonviolence, and solidarity as a world religion."[4]

II. EMPERORS AND KINGS OF THE BUDDHA'S PERIOD

During the lifetime of Sakyamuni Buddha, he received royal patronage from powerful kings and queens.

King Bimbisara of Magadha was the first to offer him a temple for residence. Bimbisara's queen, Khema, became an ardent Buddhist. After the Buddha's demise, Ajasatta, son of King Bimbisara, organized the first Buddhist conference or "sangayana" at Rajgir.[5] King Prasanjith Kosala of Sravasti (modern-day Uttar Pradesh) was a patron of Buddhism. It was at Sravasti that the Buddha spent most of the rainy seasons (Vassana).The Lichchavis of the Republic of Lichchavis (present-day Bihar) were followers of the Buddha and he reorganized their seven non-depending laws to be included in the Buddhist order.

In Kosambi under the rule of King Udeni, the first conflict among bhikkus occurred. They divided into two divisions-

---

3   Mahajan, V.D. Chand and Co. Ancient India. Ram Nagar: New Delhi, 295–298.

4   Dharmapal, Maha Thera. Ashoka – 2300. India: The Bengal Buddhist Association, Kolkata. 1997. 15, 121, 178.

5   Medhankara, Ven. Dr. Maha Thero. The Great Buddhist Emperors of Asia. Bhoomi Prakashan. Nagpur, Maharashrtra, India, 1959. 1, 41, 56, 72, 93, 100, 110, 128, 134, 146, 169, 195, 222, 234, 246, 272.

Dhamma and Vinaya.

No one can forget king Suddhodana of Kapilawattu, father of the Buddha. He paid maximum respect and veneration to Buddha. Besides Emperor Ashoka, there were other great rulers who patronized the Buddha and Buddhism in different ways. They enriched and propagated Buddhism in different parts of the world: King Dharmaraj Milinda (circa 175 BC), Emperor Kanishka (78–101 or 120 AD), and Emperor Harshawardhana (425 AD) are a few of them.

King Ansuverma of Nepal (seventh century AD), Emperor Tsrong Tsang Gampo of Tibet (617 AD), Emperor Yu Tee of Liang Dynasty China (502–549 AD), King Wang Kiyen of Korea (1340 AD), Shoroku, known as the Japanese Dharmashoka (580 AD), Dhamma Cheti of Burma (1476 AD), Emperor Dutugamunu of Sri Lanka (101–77 BC), Maha Parakramabahu of Sri Lanka (1153–1186), Emperor Kublai Khan of Mongolia (1254 AD), Sri Suryawansam of Siam (Thailand; 1355 AD), Jayaverma of Cambodia (1182–1202 AD), King Fanewn of Laos (1353 AD), King Indra Verma II of the Champa Kingdom, present-day Vietnam (860–890 AD), and Sri Vijayaag were other rulers who spread Buddhism in the above-mentioned countries.[6]

III. ASHOKA EMPEROR

Ashoka, an Indian emperor of the Maurya Dynasty who ruled almost all of the Indian subcontinent from c. 268 to 232 BC, was one of India's greatest emperors. Ashoka reigned over a realm that stretched from the Hindu Kush Mountains in Afghanistan to the modern state of Bangladesh in the east. It covered the entire Indian subcontinent except parts of present-day Tamil Nadu and Kerala. The empire's capital was Pataliputra (in Magadha, present-day Bihar), with provincial capitals at Taxila and Ujjain.

---

6   Bapat, P.V. 2500 Years of Buddhism. India: Bapat Ministry of Information and Broadcasting, Government of India, 1959. 50, 53, 56.

Around 260 BCE, Ashoka waged a bitterly destructive war against the state of Kalinga (modern Orissa). He conquered Kalinga, which none of his ancestors had done. He embraced Buddhism after witnessing the mass deaths of the Kalinga War, which he himself had waged out of a desire for conquest. Ashoka reflected on the war in Kalinga, which reportedly had resulted in more than 100,000 deaths and 150,000 deportations, ending at around 200,000 deaths. Ashoka converted gradually to Buddhism beginning about 263 BCE He was later dedicated to the propagation of Buddhism across Asia, and established monuments marking several significant sites in the life of Gautama Buddha. Ashoka regarded Buddhism as a doctrine that could serve as a cultural foundation for political unity. Ashoka is now remembered as a philanthropic administrator. In the Kalinga edicts, he addresses his people as his "children," and mentions that as a father, he desires their good.

"Aśoka" means "painless, without sorrow" in Sanskrit. In his edicts, he is referred to as Devānāmpriya (Pali: Devānaṃpiya or "Beloved of the Gods"), and Priyadarśin (Pali: Piyadasī or "He who regards everyone with affection"). His fondness for his name's connection to the Saraca asoca tree, or the "Ashoka Tree"[7] is also referenced in the Ashokavadana.

7   Bhandarakar, D.R. Aśoka, Calcutta: Calcutta University Press, 1969. 166, 230.

H.G. Wells wrote of Ashoka in his book, The Outline of History: "Amidst the tens of thousands of names of monarchs that crowd the columns of history, their majesties and graciousnesses and serenities and royal highnesses and the like, the name of Ashoka shines and shines, almost alone, a star." Along with the Edicts of Ashoka, his legend is related to the second century CE Ashokavadana ("Narrative of Ashoka," a part of the Divyavadana), and in the Sri Lankan text, Mahavamsa (Great Chronicle). The emblem of the modern Republic of India is an adaptation of the Lion Capital of Ashoka. The Dhammachakka or the wheel of Dhamma is depicted in India's national flag.

3.1. Ashoka's Early Life

Ashoka was born to the Mauryan emperor, Bindusara, and his wife, Dharmā (or Dhamma). He was the grandson of Chandragupta Maurya, founder of the Mauryan Dynasty. The Avadana texts mention that his mother was queen Subhadrangī. According to the Ashokavadana, she was the daughter of a Brahmin from the city of Champa.

Ashoka's fighting qualities were apparent from an early age, and he was given royal military training. Because of his reputation as a frightening warrior and a heartless general, he was sent to curb "the riots in the Avanti province of the Mauryan empire."[8] The Buddhist text, Divyavadana, describes Ashoka putting down a revolt due to activities of wicked ministers. This may have been an incident in Bindusara's times. Taranatha's account states that Chanakya, Bindusara's chief advisor, destroyed the nobles and kings of sixteen towns and made himself the master of all territory between the eastern and the western seas. Some historians consider this an indication of Bindusara's conquest of the Deccan, while others consider it a suppression of a revolt. Following this, Ashoka was stationed at Ujjayini as governor. Bindusara's death in 272 BC led to a war over succession. Ascending to the throne, Ashoka expanded his empire over the next eight years.

---

8   Bongard-Levin, G.M. Mauryan India. India: Stosius, 1986. 186.

3.2. Conquest of Kalinga

While the early part of Ashoka's reign was apparently quite bloodthirsty, he became a follower of the Buddha's teachings after his conquest of Kalinga on the east coast of India in the present-day states of Orissa and North Coastal Andhra Pradesh. Kalinga was a state that prided itself on its sovereignty and democracy.

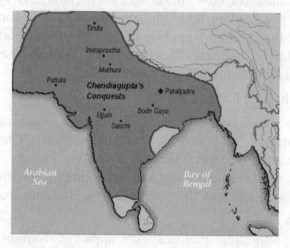

Kalinga (adjacent to the Bay of Bengal) and the Maurya Empire (blue) before the attack of Ashoka the Great

With its monarchical parliamentary democracy, it was quite an exception in ancient Bharata where there existed the concept of "Rajdharma" or "the duty of the rulers," which was intrinsically entwined with the concept of bravery and dharma. The Kalinga War happened eight years after Ashoka's coronation. From his thirteenth inscription, we know that the battle was a massive one and caused the deaths of more than 100,000 soldiers and many civilians who rose up in defense; over 150,000 were deported. When he was walking through the grounds of Kalinga after his conquest, "rejoicing in his victory, he was moved by the number of bodies strewn there and the wails of the bereaved."[9]

---

9   Aher, D.C. Ashoka the Great. Delhi: B.R. Publishers, 1995. 226, 228. https://en.wikipedia.org/wiki/Kalinga_War

3.3. Buddhist Conversion

His Majesty felt remorse at the conquest of Kalinga because during the subjugation of this previously unconquered country, slaughter, death, and kidnapping occurred, and His Majesty felt profound sorrow and regret. The edict goes on to address the even greater degree of sorrow and regret resulting from Ashoka's understanding that the friends and families of deceased would suffer greatly too. Legend says that one day after the war was over, Ashoka ventured out to roam the city and all he could see were burnt houses and scattered corpses.

The lethal war with Kalinga transformed the vengeful Emperor Ashoka to a stable and peaceful emperor and he became a patron of Buddhism. According to the prominent Indologist, A. L. Basham, Ashoka's personal religion became Buddhism, if not before, then certainly after the Kalinga war. However, according to Basham, the Dharma officially propagated by Ashoka was not Buddhism at all. Nevertheless, his patronage led to the expansion of Buddhism in the Mauryan empire and other kingdoms during his rule and worldwide from about 250 BCE.

Prominent in this cause were his son Mahinda (Mahendra) and daughter Sanghamitra (whose name means "friend of the Sangha"), who established Buddhism in Ceylon (now Sri Lanka). Information about the life and reign of Ashoka primarily comes from a relatively small number of Buddhist sources. In particular, the Sanskrit Ashokavadana (Story of Ashoka), written in the second century, and the two Pāli chronicles of Sri Lanka (the Dipavamsa and Mahavamsa), provide most of the currently known information about Ashoka. Additional information is contributed by the Edicts of Ashoka, whose authorship was finally attributed to the Ashoka of Buddhist legend after the discovery of dynastic lists that gave the name used in the edicts (Priyadarshi, "He who regards everyone with affection") as a title or additional name of Ashoka Maurya. Architectural remains of his period have been found at "Kumhrar, Patna, which include an eighty-pillar hypostyle hall."[10]

THE GREAT EMPEROR ASOKA
(304 B.C. - 232 B.C.)

King Asoka truely confessed and ceased digvijaya (conquest by war) and sought for dhammavijaya (conquest by Dhamma). He ruled his country by Buddha-Dharma with numerous good

10 Ayyar, Sulochana. Costume and Ornaments as Depicted in the Early Sculptures of Gwarlior Museum. 186.

deeds. His reign became more humane as he ruled according to the Dhamma. He was the first king to build major edicts with Buddhist inscriptions all over India and Central Asia. He set up a department of religious officers to look into moral education for the people. He went on dhammayatra (pilgrimages) to the holy places. He was generous with the requisites for the Sangha and supported them handsomely. He claimed to his neighbours that he had no expansionist intentions towards countries bordering his empire. After the Third Buddhist Council, missionary work to the adjacent nine countries saw the spread of Theravada Buddhism under his patronage. The nine countries are Kashmir and Gandhara (N. Punjab), Mahisamandala (South of Vindhyan mountains), Vanavasi (N. Kanara), Aparantaka (N. Gujarat, Kathiawar, Kacch and Sind), Maharattha (country of the Marathi, modern Bombay), Yona countries (clans of foreign race on NW frontier, Greeco-Bactrian kingdom), Himavanta (Himalayan region), Suvannabhumi (Lower Myanmar, Thailand, Java, and even Malaya) and Tambapanni (Sri Lanka) and so on.[11]

Ashoka spent lots of wealth for religious education, building monasteries and monuments. He also built the great stupa of Sanchi. He erected several thousand Buddhist monuments to enshrine the Buddha's relics. He built viharas for the monks and the famous vihara in Pataliputra was named after him, Asokarama. He also helped to develop viharas (intellectual hubs) such as Nalanda and Taxila in addition to constructing Sanchi and Mahabodhi Temple. He was the great support for the cause of the Triple Gem.

3.4. Edicts of Ashoka

The Edicts of Ashoka are a collection of thirty-three inscriptions on the Pillars of Ashoka, as well as on boulders and cave walls, made by Ashoka during his reign. These inscriptions are dispersed throughout modern-day Pakistan and India and represent the first tangible evidence of Buddhism. The edicts describe in detail the first wide expansion of Buddhism through the sponsorship of one of the

---

11   http://www.suttas.com/king-asoka.html

most powerful kings of Indian history, offering more information about "Ashoka's proselytism, moral precepts, religious precepts, and his notions of social and animal welfare."[12]

His pronouncements were written on rocks in the periphery of his kingdom, while pillars were erected along the main roads, and where pilgrims gather. Asoka's edicts were written in his own words. Asoka's edicts were found in more than thirty places throughout India, Nepal, Pakistan, and Afghanistan. Most of them were written in the native language of the place.

Asoka was engaged in spreading Buddhism through the rock, stone and pillar edicts erected in his empire and beyond. The Bhabru inscription called upon his people to respect and have faith in Buddha, Dhamma and Sangha. The individual morality that Asoka hoped to foster included respect towards parents, elders, teachers, friends, servants, ascetics and Brahmins. Girnar Rock Edict Three stressed filial duties.

He also encouraged generosity (dana), harmlessness towards life (avihimsa bhutanam), moderation in spending and saving, treating others properly and to be well learned in others' religions. The qualities of heart that are recommended by Asoka in the edicts indicate his deep spirituality. They include kindness, self-examination, truthfulness, gratitude, purity of heart, enthusiasm, loyalty, self- control and love of Dhamma. The following seven Buddhist texts were encouraged for both sangha and lay disciples. These texts favoured by Asoka appeared to bear on the life of the monks, and the ethical standards to which Asoka was devoted. Asoka did not concern himself with the philosophy of Buddhism but with the ethical and practical application.

Munigatha is praised as the recluse who goes alone to find calm, annihilating further existences, strong in understanding, virtue and concentration. The Mauneya Sutta praises the calm and detachment of recluseship. The Rahulovada Sutta is where Buddha admonishes Rahula against conscious false speech. Upatissapasine

---

12   Gokhale, Balkrishna Govind. Ashoka Maurya. USA: Irvington Publishers, 1966. 223, 228, 231.

is where Sariputta asked many questions.[13]

3.5. Ashoka-vadana Text (the Legend of Ashoka)

The Ashoka-vadana is a second-century CE text related to the legend of Ashoka. The legend was translated into Chinese by Fa Hien in 300 CE. It is essentially a Hinayana text, and its world is that of Mathura and northwest India. The emphasis of this little-known text is on exploring the relationship between the king and the community of monks (the Sangha) and setting up an ideal of religious life for the laity (the common person) by telling appealing stories about religious exploits. The most startling feature is that Ashoka's conversion has nothing to do with the Kalinga War, which is not even mentioned, nor is there a word about his belonging to the Maurya Dynasty. Equally surprising is the record of his use of state power to spread Buddhism in an uncompromising fashion. The legend of Veetashoka provides insights into Ashoka's character that are not available in the widely known Pali records.

Ashoka Pillar in Lumbini (the birthplace of Buddha), Nepal

3.6. Animal Welfare

Ashoka's rock edicts declare that injuring living things is not

---

13   http://www.suttas.com/king-asoka.html

good, and no animal should be sacrificed for slaughter. However, he did not prohibit common cattle slaughter or beef eating.

The reign of Ashoka Maurya might have disappeared into history as the ages passed by, had he not left behind records of his reign. These records are in the form of sculpted pillars and rocks inscribed with a variety of actions and teachings he wished to be published under his name. The language used for inscription was in one of the Prakrit "common" languages etched in a Brahmi script.

King Ashoka, the third monarch of the Indian Mauryan dynasty, is also considered as "one of the most exemplary rulers who ever lived." [14]

3.7. Buddhist Kingship

One of the more enduring legacies of Ashoka Maurya was the model that he provided for the relationship between Buddhism and the state. Throughout Theravada southeastern Asia, the model of rulership embodied by Ashoka replaced the notion of divine kingship that had previously dominated (in the Angkor Kingdom, for instance). Under this model of "Buddhist kingship," the king sought to legitimize his rule not through descent from a divine source, but by supporting and earning the approval of the Buddhist Sangha.

Following Ashoka's example, kings established monasteries, funded the construction of stupas, and supported the ordination of monks in their kingdom. Many rulers also took an active role in resolving disputes over the status and regulation of the sangha, as Ashoka had when he called a conclave to settle a number of contentious issues during his reign. This development ultimately led to a close association in many Southeast Asian countries between the monarchy and the religious hierarchy, an association that can still be seen today in the state-supported Buddhism of Thailand and the traditional role of the Thai king as both a religious and secular leader. Ashoka also said that all his courtiers always governed the people in a moral manner.

---

14   Nikam, N.A. and McKeon Richard. The Edicts of Ashoka. Chicago: Chicago University Press, 1959. 47, 52.

3.8. Historical Archaeological Sources on Ashoka

Ashoka and other Buddhist figures were almost forgotten by the historians of early British India, but James Prinsep contributed to the revelation of historical sources. Another important historian was British archaeologist John Hubert Marshall, who was Director-General of the Archaeological Survey of India. His main interests were Sanchi and Sarnath, in addition to Harappa and Mohenjodaro. Sir Alexander Cunningham, a British archaeologist and army engineer, and often known as the father of the Archaeological Survey of India, unveiled heritage sites like the Bharhut Stupa, Sarnath, Sanchi, and the Mahabodhi Temple. Mortimer Wheeler, a British archaeologist, also exposed Ashokan historical sources, especially the Taxila.

Bilingual inscriptions (in Greek and Aramaic) by King Ashoka were discovered at Kandahar (National Museum of Afghanistan).

The inscriptions of Ashoka's edicts

He imposed a ban on killing of "all four-footed creatures that are neither useful nor edible," and of specific animal species including several birds, and certain types of fish and bulls, among others. He also banned the killing of female goats, sheep and pigs that were nursing their young; as well as up to the age of six months. He also "banned killing of all fish and castration of animals during certain periods such as Chaturmasa and Uposatha."[15]

Ashoka also abolished the royal hunting of animals and restricted the slaying of animals for food in the royal residence. Because he banned hunting, created many veterinary clinics, and eliminated meat eating on many holidays, the Mauryan Empire under Ashoka has been described as one of the very few instances in world history of a government treating its animals as citizens who are as deserving of its protection as the human residents.

3.9. Pillars of Ashoka (Ashokastambha)

The pillars of Ashoka are "a series of columns dispersed throughout the northern Indian subcontinent and erected by Ashoka during his reign in the third century BCE."13 Originally, there must have been many pillars of Ashoka although only ten with inscriptions still survive. Averaging between forty and fifty feet in height, and weighing up to fifty tons each, all the pillars were quarried at Chunar, just south of Varanasi and dragged, sometimes hundreds of miles, to where they were erected.

National Emblem and Flag of India

---

15   Dharmapal, Maha Thera. Ashoka–2300. Kolkata, India: The Bengal Buddhist Association, 1997. 70, 72.

The first Pillar of Ashoka was found in the sixteenth century by Thomas Cory in the ruins of ancient Delhi. The wheel represents the sun time and Buddhist law, while the swastika stands for the cosmic dance around a fixed center and guards against evil. The Lion Capital of Ashoka is a sculpture of four lions standing back-to-back. It was originally placed atop the Ashoka pillar at Sarnath, now in the state of Uttar Pradesh, India. The pillar, sometimes called the Ashoka Column, is still in its original location, but the Lion Capital is now in the Sarnath Museum.

This Lion Capital of Ashoka from Sarnath has been adopted as the National Emblem of India and the wheel "Ashoka Chakra" from its base was placed onto the center of the National Flag of India. The capital contains four lions (Indian/Asiatic Lions), standing back-to-back, mounted on an abacus, with a frieze carrying sculptures in high relief of an elephant, a galloping horse, a bull, and a lion, separated by intervening spoked chariot wheels over a bell-shaped lotus. Carved out of a single block of polished sandstone, the capital was believed to be crowned by a "Wheel of Dharma" ("Dharmachakra," popularly known in India as the "Ashoka Chakra").

The Ashoka Lion Capital or the Sarnath Lion Capital is also known as the national symbol of India. The Sarnath pillar bears one of the Edicts of Ashoka, an inscription against division within the Buddhist community, which reads, "No one shall cause division in the order of monks." The Sarnath pillar is a column surmounted by a capital, which consists of a canopy representing an inverted bell-shaped lotus flower, a short cylindrical abacus with four twenty-four-spoked Dharma wheels with four animals (an elephant, a bull, a horse, a lion).The four animals in the Sarnath Capital are believed to symbolize different steps of Lord Buddha's life.The Ashoka Lion capital is displayed at the Archaeological Museum in Sarnath. It is India's national emblem; the national symbol is used in almost all the government documents since ancient times.

The Elephant represents the Buddha's idea in reference to the dream of Queen Maya of a white elephant entering her womb.

- The Bull represents desire during the life of the Buddha as a prince.

- The Horse represents Buddha's departure from palatial life.

- The Lion represents the accomplishment of the Buddha.

Besides the religious interpretations, there are some non-religious interpretations of the symbolism of the Ashoka Capital Pillar at Sarnath. According to them, "the four lions symbolize Ashoka's rule over the four directions; the wheels as symbols of his enlightened rule (Chakravartin) and the four animals are symbols of four adjoining territories of India."[16]

Following is the Dhamma law of piety instilled by Ashoka during his religious administration meant for a nonviolent and peaceful society:

1. Samyam or mastery of senses

2. Bhavasuddhi or purity of thought

3. Kritajnata or gratitude

4. Dridh-bhakti or steadfastness of devotion

---

16 Chauhan, Giand Chand, Origin and Growth of Feudalism in Early India: From the Mauryas to AD 650. Delhi: Munshiram Manoharlal Publishers, 2004. 186, 192. Mahajan, V.D. Kalinga Rock Edicts–Ancient India. New Delhi: S. Chand and Co. 2008. Ltd. Publishers. 300, 304.

5. Daya or kindness

6. Dana or charity

7. Saucha or purity

8. Satya or truthfulness

9. Sushrust or service

10. Sampritipatti or support

11. Apichiti or support (Kalinga Rock Edict xii and xiii).[17]

Ashoka Pillars: a series of columns that are dispersed throughout the Indian subcontinent and carry inscriptions addressed to monks and nuns. Of all the pillars erected by him, there are only twenty of them that still survive. Out of these twenty, only seven well-preserved animal sculptures are present.[18]

3.10. Death and Legacy

Ashoka's Major Rock Edict at Junagadh contains inscriptions by Ashoka (fourteen of the Edicts of Ashoka), Rudradaman I, and Skandagupta. Ashoka ruled for an estimated thirty-six years. Legend states that during his cremation, his body burned for seven days and nights. After his death, the Mauryan Dynasty lasted just fifty more years until his empire stretched over almost all of the

17   Kiskalar, D.B. "Literary Value of Inscriptions of Ashoka," Journal of Indian History. New Delhi. 226.
18   https://fairgaze.com/fgnews/the-pillars-of-ashoka_92319.html

Indian subcontinent.

Ashoka had many wives and children, but many of their names are lost to time. His chief consort (agramahisi) for the majority of his reign was his wife, Asandhimitra, who apparently bore him no children. In his old age, he seems to have come under the spell of his youngest wife, Tishyaraksha. It is said that she had Ashoka's son Kunala, the regent in Takshashila and the heir presumptive to the throne, blinded by a wily stratagem. The official executioners spared Kunala and he became a wandering singer accompanied by his favorite wife, Kanchanmala. In Pataliputra, Ashoka heard Kunala's song, and realized that Kunala's misfortune may have been a punishment for some past sin of the emperor himself. He condemned Tishyaraksha to death, restoring Kunala to the court. In the Ashokavadana, Kunala is portrayed as forgiving Tishyaraksha, having obtained enlightenment through Buddhist practice. While he urges "Ashoka to forgive her as well, Ashoka does not respond with the same forgiveness. Kunala was succeeded by his son, Samprati, who ruled for fifty years until his death."[19]

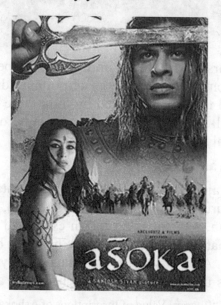

---

19   Bandarkar, B.R. Ashoka. Kolkata. Calcutta University, 1999. 87, 89.

Asoka, is the Indian Hindi-language epic historical drama film from 2001, in which the famous star, Shah Rukh Khan, played the role of Ashoka with actress Kareena Kapoor playing his wife. The film describes that Emperor Asoka was one of the great moral reformers in the history of civilization and a precocious pioneer of humanitarian values.

IV. HISTORY OF VIETNAM AND BUDDHISM

4.1. First Human Evidence

Archaeological excavations have revealed the existence of humans in what is now Vietnam as early as the Paleolithic Age. "Homo erectus fossils dating to around 500,000 BC have been found in caves in Lạng Sơn and Nghệ An Provinces in northern Vietnam."[20]

4.2. Paleolithic to Neolithic

By about 1000 BC, the development of wet-rice cultivation and bronze casting in the Ma River and Red River floodplains led to the flourishing of the Đông Sơn culture, notable for its elaborate bronze drums. At this time, "the early Vietnamese kingdoms of Văn Lang and Âu Lạc appeared, and the culture's influence spread to other parts of Southeast Asia, including Maritime Southeast Asia throughout the first millennium BC."16

People appeared in Vietnam about 10,000–30,000 years ago with vestiges of the Núi Đọ, Thần Sa, Sơn Vi. New Age was typical with Hòa Bình, Bắc Sơn cultures about 6,000–10,000 years ago and the Metal Age was about 4,000 years ago.

4.3. The National Name of Vietnam

Kinh Dương Vương is the ancestor of the Vietnamese nation. The Văn Lang country lasted for nearly 2,000 years, through eighteen Hùng kings and the capital was located in Phong Châu.

---

20 https://www.indochinavalue.com/vietnam-travel-guide/vietnamese-history/prehistoric-vietnam
https://giaoduc.net.vn/ten-goi-viet-nam-co-tu-khi-nao-post189425.gd

The Thục Dynasty (257–208 BC) took the country name Âu Lạc, stationed the capital in Cổ Loa. The Triệu Dynasty (207–111 BC) occupied Âu Lạc, and changed the country's name to Nam Việt. The Hán Dynasty (111 BC–39) occupied Nam Việt and changed it to Giao Chỉ. "Vietnam," the national name of Vietnam officially appeared in the Nguyễn Dynasty and was proclaimed in 1804. When the August Revolution of 1945 succeeded on September 2, 1945, when "President Hồ Chí Minh read the Declaration of Independence giving birth to the Democratic Republic of Vietnam (Việt Nam Dân chủ Cộng hòa), the national name of Vietnam was officially recognized."

Vietnam was part of Imperial China for over a millennium, from 111 BC to AD 939. An independent Vietnamese state was formed in 939, following a Vietnamese victory in the Battle of Bạch Đằng River. Successive Vietnamese royal dynasties flourished as the nation expanded geographically and politically into Southeast Asia, until the Indochina Peninsula was colonized by the French in the mid-nineteenth century.

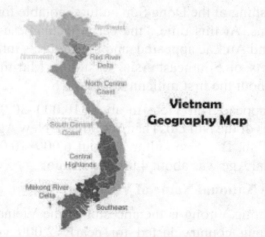

Vietnam Geography Map

Following a Japanese occupation in the 1940s, the Vietnamese fought French rule in the First Indochina War, eventually expelling the French in 1954. Thereafter, Vietnam was divided politically into two rival states, North and South Vietnam. Conflict between the two sides intensified in what is known as the Vietnam War. The war ended with a North Vietnamese victory in 1975.

Vietnam was then unified but remained impoverished and politically isolated. In 1986, Vietnam carried out economic renovation and foreign policy reform with the motto of wanting to be friends with all countries. As a result, Vietnam's economy, politics, and society has become more and more stable and developed. Currently, Vietnam is enjoying peace after a long history of struggle to build and defend the country.

4.4. Buddhism in Vietnam

Buddhism in Vietnam (in Vietnamese called đạo Phật or Phật giáo) as practiced by the ethnic Vietnamese is mainly of the Mahāyāna tradition. Buddhism may have first come to Vietnam as early as the third or second century BCE from South Asia or from China in the first or second century CE. Vietnamese Buddhism has had a symbiotic relationship with certain elements of Taoism, Chinese spirituality, and the Vietnamese folk religion.

Indian Prime Minister N. D. Modi visited Quán Sứ Temple in Hà Nội in 2016

There are conflicting theories regarding whether Buddhism first reached Vietnam during the third or second century BCE via delegations from India, or during the first or second century from China. In either case, by the end of the second century CE, Vietnam had developed into a major regional Mahāyāna Buddhist center centering on Luy Lâu in modern Bắc Ninh Province, northeast of the present-day capital city of Hanoi. Luy Lâu was the capital of the Hán region of Jiaozhi (Giao Chỉ) and was a popular place visited by many Indian Buddhist missionary monks en route to China. The monks followed "the maritime trade route from the Indian sub-continent to China used by Indian traders. A number of Mahāyāna sutras and the āgamas were translated into Classical Chinese there, including the Sutra of Forty-Two Chapters and the Anapanasati Sutra."[21]

Over the next eighteen centuries, Vietnam and China shared many common features of cultural, philosophical, and religious heritage. This was due to geographical proximity and Vietnam being annexed twice by China. Vietnamese Buddhism is thus related to Chinese Buddhism in general, and to some extent reflects the formation of Chinese Buddhism after the Song Dynasty.

Theravāda Buddhism, on the other hand, would become incorporated through the southern annexation of Khmer people and territories. During the Đinh Dynasty (968–980), Buddhism was recognized by the state as an official faith (971), reflecting the high esteem of Buddhist faith held by the Vietnamese monarchs. The Early Lê dynasty (980–1009) also afforded the same recognition to the Buddhist church. The growth of Buddhism during this time is attributed to the recruitment of erudite monks to the court as the newly independent state needed an ideological basis on which to build a country. Subsequently, this role was ceded to Confucianism. Vietnamese Buddhism reached its zenith during the Lý dynasty (1009–1225) beginning with the founder Lý Thái Tổ, who was raised in a pagoda. All of the kings during the Lý dynasty professed

21 Nguyễn Lang (aka Zen Master Thích Nhất Hạnh), Việt Nam Phật giáo Sử luận, tập 1,2,3. 1973.
    https://langmai.org/tang-kinh-cac/vien-sach/giang-kinh/viet-nam-phat-giao-su-luan/chuong-
12-tran-nhan-tong-va-thien-phai-truc-lam/

and sanctioned Buddhism as the state religion. This endured with "the Trần Dynasty (1225–1400) but Buddhism had to share the stage with the emerging growth of Confucianism."[22]

By the fifteenth century, Buddhism fell out of favor with the court during the later Lê dynasty, although still popular with the masses. Officials like Lê Quát attacked it as heretical and wasteful. It was not until the nineteenth century that Buddhism regained some stature under the Nguyễn dynasty who accorded royal support.

The Thiền school, founded by King Trần Nhân Tông (1258–1308), was named the Trúc Lâm (meaning "Bamboo Grove" Zen sect). This revealed a deep influence of Confucian and Taoist philosophy. Nevertheless, Trúc Lâm's prestige waned over the following centuries as Confucianism became dominant in the royal court. In the seventeenth century, a group of Chinese monks, led by Nguyên Thiều, introduced the Ling school (Lâm Tế). A more domesticated offshoot of Lâm Tế, the Liễu Quán school was founded in the eighteenth century and has since been a branch of Vietnamese Zen. Since the twentieth and twenty-first century Zen Master Thích Thanh Từ has been restored to the Trúc Lâm Zen Sect by founding hundreds of Trúc Lâm Zen monasteries in Vietnam and abroad, especially the predominant Yên Tử Mount (Quảng Ninh) where the Trần Nhân Tông Zen founder resided and spread the Vietnamese Zen.

Buddhism has been present in Vietnam for over 2,600 years, associated with the ups and downs of the nation's destiny, from the time of Hùng Vương, Chư Đồng Tử – Tiên Dung, Hai Bà Trưng, Ngô Quyền, Lý Dynasty (1010–1225), Trần reign (1225–1400), Lê Dynasty (1418–1527), Trịnh-Nguyễn (1533–1788), Nguyễn (1802–1883), and Pháp đô hộ (1883–1945) to currently. Buddhism with its moral doctrine of doing good, avoiding evil, and keeping the mind pure still exist in the nation as poet Huyền Không said:

---

22 Lê Văn Hưu, Phan Phu Tiên, Ngô Sĩ Liên. Đại Việt Sử Ký Toàn Thư (National Bureau for Historical Records). 1993, P. 182. Viện Khoa Học Xã Hội Việt Nam dịch (1985–1992).
https://www.tuvienquangduc.com.au/lichsu/lichsuvietnam/Daivietsukytoanthu.pdf

The roof of the pagoda protects the soul of the nation
It is the eternal living way of our ancestors.

(Remember the Pagoda – Huyền Không)
(Mái Chùa che chở hồn dân tộc
Nếp sống muôn đời của tổ tiên.
Nhớ Chùa – Huyền Không)

Especially through the dynasties of Đinh, Lê, Lý, Trần, Trịnh, Nguyễn... Buddhism developed to its peak and many monks became the National Masters for the Vietnamese Kings, advising and planning national development programs such as Venerable Khuông Việt, the chief of Sangha, Ngô Chân Lưu, Zen Master Vạn Hạnh, the skilled Zen poet Tuệ Trung Thượng Sỹ, King Trần Thái Tông, the Trúc Lâm Zen Founder – King Trần Nhân Tông, and so on.

V. TRẦN NHÂN TÔNG EMPEROR (1258–1308)

5.1. Since Childhood, He Had the Golden Buddha Signs

Trần Nhân Tông, the third emperor of the Trần Dynasty of Vietnam, was born on December 7, 1258 (Novermber 11 of the Lunar Calender 1258). His birth name was Trần Khâm. He was the first son of the Emperor Trần Thánh Tông.[23]

---

23   Việt Nam Phật Giáo Sử Luận (History of Vietnam Buddhism), tập 1,2,3. Nguyễn Lang (aka Zen Master Thích Nhất Hạnh), Lá Bối. 1973. https://langmai.org/tang-kinh-cac/vien-sach/giang-kinh/viet-nam-phat-giao-su-luan/chuong-12-tran-nhan-tong-va-thien-phai-truc-lam/

The Golden Buddha Trần Nhân Tông, the first Trúc Lâm Zen Founder

It was said that the newborn Trần Khâm had the elite sign of the saints, such as the pure gold physique and the bright perfect manner. Both signs are considered signs of a heavenly extraordinary appearance. His grandfather Thái Tông and father Thánh Tông named him "Kim Tiên Đồng Tử (Pupil of the Heaven)."[24] Due to these good generals, he was also honored as "the Golden Buddha" (Phật Hoàng), Phật Hoàng Trần Nhân Tông ever since he was a child.

5.2. Wanting to Give Up His Position as King and Become a Monastic

Prince Trần Khâm was entitled as crown prince of the Trần Dynasty in December 1274 (sixteen years old). The Emperor himself also composed poems and a literary work called Di Hậu Lục (Two Books). He taught the crown prince how to behave in order to prepare for the future king and the faiths, so the prince became a master of the Three Religions (Buddhism, Taoism, and Confucianism). However, Trần Khâm was fond of a Buddhist life and had followed Zen since his childhood. At the age of sixteen,

---

24 Book *Tam Tổ Thực Lục* called "The Golden Buddha" (Phật Hoàng). Ibid. https://langmai.org/tang-kinh-cac/vien-sach/giang-kinh/viet-nam-phat-giao-su-luan/chuong-12-tran-nhan-tong-va-thien-phai-truc-lam/

he was anointed crown prince. He tried to "yield the royal role to his younger brother but his father King Trần Thánh Tông refused his attempt."[25]

His father king Trần Thánh Tông forced his crown prince son to marry the eldest daughter of Nguyên Từ Quốc Mẫu. His wife later had the title of Khâm Tộ Thái Hậu.

In the royal palace with his wife, he lived in comfort and happiness but always thought of leading an ascetic life by becoming a monk. One must remember that this was the same grand thinking and ambition that prince Siddharta had to lead a non-attached, non-worldly life. Further, like Prince Siddharta he left his royal palace in search of truth at midnight of a full moon day, leaving his wife Yasodhara and child Rahula. This is known as the great renunciation. The prince later became Sakyamuni Buddha, the Enlightened One. Trần Nhân Tông also, "One night at the time of the Rat, climbed out of the citadel, which had most comforts of the world, and fled towards Yên Tử mountain. There he approached Tháp Temple at the Đông Cứu Mountain. When it was morning, he immediately went to hide in the tower and lay down for a rest."[26]

The head monk of the temple made a meal for the guest as the stranger had an extraordinary appearance. The head monk recognized him and sent the message to the king. The army unit deployed by the king traced him and made him return to the palace. So due to his father and the sense of heavy duty for country, the prince returned to the worldly life to keep the royal lineage.

5.3. Even as King, He Kept a Vegetarian Diet and Practiced Zen

At the age of twenty-one (in 1279), he was crowned emperor, alias Trần Nhân Tông. Although in a noble position, he still kept himself pure, vegtarian, eating one time a day at noon and he often went to Từ Phước pagoda to practice.

---

25 Lê Văn Hưu, Phan Phu Tiên, Ngô Sĩ Liên. 1993. 18.
26 Lê Văn Hưu, Phan Phu Tiên, Ngô Sĩ Liên. 1993. 195.

In the year of leaving home, the king invited Văn Túc Vương Đạo Tái (son of Trần Quang Khải) to join him for lunch. Being very fond of Văn Túc Vương Đạo Tái, the king invited Dao Tai to vist at Dưỡng Đức building in Thánh Từ Palace and sent a person to serve the dishes to invite Đạo Tái. The king was already a vegetarian, so he just sat and watched Đạo Tái eating the non-vegetarian meal. The king wrote the following poem:

The meat is crimson token

The dish smells and looks taste

I am a mountain monk who keeps pure precepts

Sitting together but not eating together.

(Món quy cước đỏ thắm

Món mã yên vàng thơm

Sơn tăng giữ tịnh giới

Cùng ngồi không cùng ăn)[27]

Even if the king hadn't ordained, he still considered himself a "mountain monk." He cherished his will to be a monastic and prepared for his ordination.

There was another significant event in his life. One day on lunch break, he dreamed that in his navel grew a golden lotus the size of a wheel, on which there was a golden Buddha. Someone stood beside him and said, "Do you know this Buddha? That's the Virtue Transformation!". When he woke up, he brought it up to his father, King Thánh Tông, who cried and persuaded his son to live the royal life, to postpone his monastic life as below:

---

27   Việt Nam Phật Giáo Sử Luận (History of Vietnam Buddhism), tập 1,2,3. Nguyễn Lang (aka Zen Master Thích Nhất Hạnh), Lá Bối. 1973. https://langmai.org/tang-kinh-cac/vien-sach/giang-kinh/viet-nam-phat-giao-su-luan/chuong-12-tran-nhan-tong-va-thien-phai-truc-lam/

The Book of Tam Tổ Thực Lục[28] says: "Although he sat on nine layers of glorious pedestals, his life was very pure. One day napping at Từ Phước pagoda in the inner city, King Trần Nhân Tông dreamed that on his navel bloomed a lotus as large as a wheel, on which was a golden Buddha. Beside him, someone pointed to the king and asked: Do you know this Buddha? That's the Virtue Transformation! The king woke up, brought the dream back to Thánh Tông, and everyone was surprised. Ever since, he was often vegetarian to avoid meat and fish, and his face was so emaciated. Thánh Tông found his son, who still favored the monastic life, cried and said: 'I am old, I rely on you alone, if you are like that, how can I continue the prosperity of my ancestors?' King Trần Nhân Tông also cried and he accepted to keep the throne while learning Buddhism."[29]

He was compassionate, insightful, and multitalented, reading all kinds of scriptures through both internal (Buddhist studies) and secular texts, and often inviting Buddhist masters to come and lecture on Zen studies. He also consulted with Tuệ Trung Thượng Sĩ, and thus penetrated the essence of Zen, so he often took his humble position of a disciple to treat Tuệ Trung as his teacher.

5.4. Three Times Victories over Mongolian–Yuan Invaders to Protect Country

The Emperor Trần Nhân Tông and his father, the retired Emperor Trần Thánh Tông, were credited as the supreme commanders who led the Trần Dynasty to the three victories over Mongolian (Mông) and Chinese Yuan (Nguyên) invaders and established a long period of peace and prosperity over the country.

Firstly, the Mongols attacked Đại Việt in February 1258. From Đại Lý, about 15,000–25,000 Mongol cavalry and 20,000 Đại Lý troops (a total of about 35,000–45,000 men) entered Đại Việt.

---

28   Việt Nam Phật Giáo Sử Luận (History of Vietnam Buddhism), tập 1,2,3. Nguyễn Lang (aka Zen Master Thích Nhất Hạnh), Lá Bối. 1973. https://langmai.org/tang-kinh-cac/vien-sach/giang-kinh/viet-nam-phat-giao-su-luan/chuong-12-tran-nhan-tong-va-thien-phai-truc-lam/
29   Ibid.

Secondly, twenty-seven years later, the Yuan Emperor Kublai Khan (Hốt Tất Liệt) ordered the invasion of Đại Việt. This war lasted from the end of December of the Monkey Year to the end of April of the year of the Rooster (the end of January to the end of May 1285 of the solar calendar). This time, the Yuan army prepared for the war better, mobilizing a much larger force, up to tens of thousands of troops. In addition to the army coming down from the north, there were also marines from the Chiêm Thành front in the south to support.

Thirdly, immediately after the defeat, returning China in 1287, the Yuan army reorganized and supplemented their forces to take revenge. Learning from previous defeats, the Yuan forces built many food ships by sea to return to fight Đại Việt for the third time. This war lasted about four months, from the end of December 1287 to the end of April 1288.

In the beginning of the war, Thánh Tông and Nhân Tông had to order the skilled army to retreat to avoid the pressure from Yuan's force when Prince Chiêu Minh Trần Quang Khải commanded troops try to stop Sogetu's fleet in the Nghệ An Province. During this time, there were several high-ranking officials and members of royal family of the Trần Dynasty who defected to Yuan's side, including Thánh Tông's own brother, Prince Chiêu Quốc Trần Ích Tắc, and Trần Kiện who was son of Prince Tĩnh Quốc Trần Quốc Khang.

Dealing with the threat from the north, in October 1282, the retired Emperor Trần Thánh Tông and the Emperor Trần Nhân Tông gathered all members of the royal family and officials in the royal court to discuss the unadvoidable war. In 1283, Hưng Đạo Vương (real name Trần Quốc Tuấn) was appointed as "commander-in-chief (Quốc công Tiết Chế) of Đại Việt Army, and the retired Emperor and the Emperor began to hold military exercises with their generals and troops."[30]

To build the whole nation into a strong national resistance the

---

30   Lê Văn Hưu, Phan Phu Tiên, Ngô Sĩ Liên. 1993. 195.

emperor listened to the ideas from experienced persons. He held a conference of the military generals at Bình Than, and then a conference of the old sages at Diên Hồng. For example, under the smart plan of Nhân Tông. "In the Horse Year, fourth year [1282], in the winter, in October, King Nhân Tông went to Bình Than to stay in Trần Xá village to meet the royal court and hundreds of mandarins, to discuss skillfully crafting plans and dividing up to keep dangerous places wisely."

The first invasion of the Mongols was just stone-throwing. Despite being smashed by the Trần Dynasty, the greatest danger was still there. Thirty years later, the giant army of invaders on both land and water of the Yuan Mongolian Empire, at its peak after knocking down the Southern Song Dynasty, entered our country with an imperceptible momentum, and we could not resist. However, a benevolent Zen master Nhân Tông' Kind who did not want to be a king, along with his small army, calmly defeated the Chinese and Mongolian army of "the wrath of God."[31]

On May 10 of the lunar calendar 1285, Trần Quang Khải fought the decisive battle in Chương Dương where Sogetu's navy was almost destroyed and therefore the balance in the battlefield tilted definitely in favor of the Trần Dynasty. Ten days after Sogetu was killed and Trần's Emperor Nhân Tông and retired Emperor Thánh Tông returned to the capital of Thăng Long on June 6 of lunar calendar, 1285.

In March 1287, the Yuan dynasty launched their third invasion of Đại Việt. Unlike the second attack, this time Commander in Chief Hưng Đạo Vương (Trần Quốc Tuấn) affirmed with the emperor that Đại Việt's army could easily break Yuan's military campaign. Indeed, this invasion was ended one year later by a disastrous defeat of the Yuan Navy at the Battle of Bạch Đằng on March 8 of lunar calendar, 1288. Besides Trần Quốc Tuấn, other notable generals of the Trần dynasty during this time were Nhân Huệ Vương (Trần Khánh Dư) who destroyed the logistics convoy of the Yuan Navy in the Battle of Vân Đồn or general Phạm Ngũ

31   https://vi.wikipedia.org/wiki/Chi%E1%BA%BFn_tranh_Nguyen-Mong

Lão, who took charge of ambushing Prince Toghan's retreating troops.

The critical situation of the Trần dynasty began to change after their victory in the Battle of Hàm Tử in April 1285, where the troops commanded by Trần Nhật Duật, Prince Chiêu Thành, Trần Quốc Toản, and Nguyễn Khoái were finally able to defeat the fleet of Sogetu. In rewarding the Trần Dynasty generals and mandarins after the victory, "Thánh Tông and Nhân Tông also reminded them to be cautious of the northern border." [32]

The Monglian Yuan-Đại Việt War or the Resistance War against the Mongol invaders was a war to protect the Fatherland of Đại Việt troops and people in the early Trần Dynasty under the Trần Thánh Tông and Trần Nhân Tông kings. Although the time of the resistance war was from 1258 to 1288, the official war time only included about nine months in total, divided into three phases of the first, second, and third wars which were the times of active diplomacy. As a result, these three resistance wars are considered as one of the most heroic historical pages of the Vietnamese nation, and also a typical feat of the Trần Dynasty.

Ever since, it can be said Nhân Tông was a true Buddhist cultivator with widespread compassion, and also a wise hero in Vietnam history. Not only did he manage the country strongly,

32 Chapuis. 1995. 84–85. 32. Ngô Sĩ Liên. 1993.19

defeating two invasions of the most terrible Mongolian Army in the world, but he also expanded the territory of two continents for Vietnam as well as deepening his spiritual practice.

5.5. Trần Nhân Tông King Became a Monk and Founder of Trúc Lâm Zen School

In 1293, Trần Nhân Tông yielded the kingship to his son, Trần Anh Tông, and mentored the new king for six years. In 1299, he entered the monkhood at Ngọa Vân Am, in the bamboo forest on Yên Tử Mountain where he practiced strictly as a twelve-ascetic precept-holder,[33] so He was called "A Great Ascetic of Fragrant Clouds (means Hương Vân Đại Đầu Đà)."[34]

Some time after ordination, Hương Vân Đại Đầu Đà founded the Trúc Lâm (Bamboo Grove) Zen School on Yên Tử Mount. It is the only native school of Buddhism in Vietnam showing influences from Confucian and Taoist philosophy. This is a type of worldly Buddhist Zen as he was still engaged the politics of the royal court and still maintained his spiritual practice (secular and supersecular at the same time). He became the sixth patriarch of the Yên Tử Sect and the first ancestor of the Trúc Lâm Zen Sect. He also had other names such as Trúc Lâm, Great Ascetic (Trúc Lâm Đại Đầu Đà), Trúc Lâm Great Monk (Trúc Lâm Đại Sĩ) and the Golden Buddha Controller (Giác Hoàng Điều Ngự).[35]

In Yên Tử Mount, he opened a vihara, lectured for monastics, and gained quite a number of disciples.

---

33 12 ascetic precepts: 1) Garments of cast-off rags. 2) To wear only three garments. 3) Eat only food begged. 4) Eat only breakfast and the main noon meal. 5) No food between breakfast and the noon meal. 6) Eat with limited amount, only eat what you have in the begging bowl without asking for more. 7) Dwelling as a hermit. 8) Dwelling among tombs. 9) Dwelling under a tree. 10) Dwelling under the open sky. 11) Dwelling anywhere. 12) Sitting and not lying down.

34 Lê Văn Hưu, Phan Phu Tiên, Ngô Sĩ Liên. Đại Việt Sử Ký Toàn Thư (National Bereau for Historical Record). Viện Khoa Học Xã Hội Việt Nam dịch (1985 - 1992). 1993.
https://www.tuvienquangduc.com.au/lichsu/lichsuvietnam/Daivietsukytoanthu.pdf

35 Ibid.

View of the birthplace of Trúc Lâm Zen School, Yên Tử Mount,
Quảng Ninh

Trúc Lâm Buddhism played the role as the the Engaged Buddhism, closely related to politics, culture, and society. The Trúc Lâm Buddhists were very suitable for such a movement and that is the main reason why this Zen school was founded. The Yên Tử Buddhist tradition and Trúc Lâm's appearance has brought a lot of social character and entered the world, so it is natural and reasonable to use a new title for the new sect in fourteenth-century Vietnam.

In the sixth-thirteenth centuries, Đại Việt existed mainly based on three Zen lines of Tỳ-Ni-Đa-Luu-Chi (Vinītaruci)[36] Vô Ngôn Thông[37] and Thảo Đường.[38]

---

36   In the 6th century, the Patriarch Vinītaruci went from India to China to study Buddhism with the Patriarch Tăng Xán. After attaining enlightenment, he was taught by the Patriarch Tăng Xán to go to the South to spread Zen Buddhism, so he went to Vietnam to stay at Dâu Pagoda.

37   In the 9th century, there was Zen Master Vô Ngôn Thôn, a disciple of Bá Trượng's ancestor in China, who went to Vietnam to transmit meditation, so there was Vô Ngôn ThônZen sect.

38   There was Master Thảo Đường, when the Ly dynasty conquered Champa, captured a number of officials and brought them back to Vietnam, including him. Only in Thăng Long did he discover that he was a Zen master, since then the kings and mandarins of the Lý Dynasty admired and respected him and he became the Patriarch of the Thảo Đường Zen sect in Vietnam.

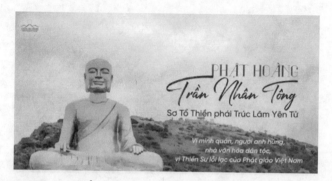

Crown Prince Trần Khâm, later King Trần Nhân Tông, was sent by King Trần Thánh Tông to Tuệ Trung Thượng Sĩ to study morality. Before returned his palace, the prince asked, "What is the main goal of meditation?" Tuệ Trung Thượng Sĩ replied, "Reflecting on self-discipline is the main duty, avoiding running outside," that is, turning back to reflect on oneself, that is the main duty to attain enlightenment, nothing else, nothing from the outside.

After enthronement, King Trần Nhân Tông both took care of the governance of the country and studied the internal scriptures, without ever neglecting either. At the throne for a while, seeing that there was an heir, at the age of forty-one, he gave all power to his son and left home. He went to Yên Tử mountain to practice. After five years of practicing asceticism in the bamboo forest, he was completely enlightened to the Way. Since then, he spread the word and founded the Trúc Lâm Yên Tử Zen Sect.

"The Trúc Lâm Yên Tử sect was born, including the three quintessences of the three sects of Vinītaruci, Vô Ngôn Thông, and Thảo Đường, agglomerating into a pure Vietnamese Zen Sect."[39] Since Trúc Lâm Yên Tử sect was born, the other sects have been absent and no longer developed. This is considered the first unified Buddhist church in Vietnam.

Trúc Lâm Zen Sect acquires "the foundation of South Asian Buddhism and Đông Độ (Indian) meditation, while

39 http://thuongchieu.net/index.php/phapthoai/suong/1960-pht-giao-thin-tong-vit-nam

using Vietnamese cultural values and encouraging Buddhists to contribute to society on the basis of the compassion and wisdom of Buddhism. Master Trúc Lâm himself not only settled in Yên Tử, but also lectured many pagodas such as Phổ Minh (Thiên Trường), Sùng Nghiêm (Chí Linh), Vĩnh Nghiêm (Yên Dũng) và Báo Ân – Siêu Loại (nay thuộc Gia Lâm, Hà Nội)."[40]

5.6. Forming a Buddhist-Based Society

To support Đại Việt and learn the scriptures of the Buddha, in the second lunar month of 1295, Master Trúc Lâm sent the foreign ministers Trần Khắc Dụng and Phạm Thảo to Yuan Chinese Dynasty to request the Great Tripitaka (Sutras, Vinaya, and Abhidharma). This request was approved by Nguyên Thành Tông. The sutras brought back by the mission were kept in Thiên Trường palace, and in addition, the emperor ordered the copy to be printed for circulation in the country.

In 1304, Master Hương Vân Đại Đầu Đà (Trần Nhân Tông) traveled around the country, encouraging his people to quit worshipping sexual gods and to abandon wrong views. He taught the ten good deeds, (1) not to kill, (2) not to steal, (3) to refrain from all sexual activity, (4) not to lie, (5) not to drink intoxicants, (6) not to wear ornaments or perfume, (7) not to listen to singing or watch dancing, (8) not to sleep on an elevated or broad bed, (9) not to eat at an improper hour, i.e., after noon, and (10) not to own valuables such as gold and silver. He still gave advice on some political issues, and advised Anh Tông King "to give up alcohol and make often offerings and supported the monks."[41]

Ten Precepts is the basic teaching of Buddhism, the basis for social ethics. Trúc Lâm had the intention to build a society on the basis of Buddhist morality. A young king sat on the throne in support of Buddhism, a king who worked as a monk to travel among the masses. This event is unique and unprecedented. Whether "consciously or not, Trúc Lâm also contributed to the consolidation of the dynasty and regime by active religious

40   https://terebess.hu/zen/mesterek/Tran-Nhan-Tong.html
41   https://terebess.hu/zen/mesterek/Tran-Nhan-Tong.html

practices in the folk."[42]

In the winter of the same year, 1304, King Trần Anh Tông requested that Master Hương Vân Đại Đầu Đà visit the royal citadel and transmit the Bodhisattva Precepts for laywomen and laymen. Aterwards, he came to reside at Sùng Nghiêm Temple in Linh Sơn Mountain, where he performed the Bodhisattva ordination and taught Zen to the general public.

The monarchs who took the bodhisattva ordination were those who vowed to use the ability and power of their royal position to serve people based on the bodhisattva's conduct. On the day Trúc Lâm Zen Master entered the citadel, the kings and officers followed the king to welcome National Master Trúc Lâm. Seeing that King Trần Anh Tông made a vow to take the bodhisattva precepts, they also took Refuge in the Triple Gem (following the way of Buddha, dharma, and sangha) and keeping Five Precepts (abstaining from killing living beings, stealing, sexual misconduct, lying and intoxication). In terms of formality, an entire court became Buddhist and a Buddhist-based society with their citizens living a moral life as their kings and ancestors.

5.7. The Second Ancestor of the Trúc Lâm Zen Sect

The first ancestor, Trúc Lâm, was an example of a talented and virtuous sangha leader and emperor. During his time traveling in the

---

42 Việt Nam Phật giáo Sử luận (History of Vietnam Buddhism), tập 1,2,3. Nguyễn Lang (aka Zen Master Thích Nhất Hạnh), Lá Bối. 1973.
https://langmai.org/tang-kinh-cac/vien-sach/giang-kinh/viet-nam-phat-giao-su-luan/chuong-12-tran-nhan-tong-va-thien-phai-truc-lam/

human world, Trúc Lâm also intended to find a dharma successor, that is, a person who could continue his career of preaching in the world.

In 1304, when he came to Nam Sách village, Trúc Lâm met a young man, twenty-one years old, who wanted to become a monk, named Đồng Kiên Cương. Seeing his unusual appearance, Trúc Lâm said to himself, "This young man has an insight vision and in the future will surely become a dharma preacher." Happy because of this meeting, Trúc Lâm named him Thiện Lai, gave him the novice ordination, and sent him to study with the Most Venerable Tính Giác. Thiện Lai later became Pháp Loa, the second patriarch of the Trúc Lâm Zen Sect.

Pháp Loa only worked as a novice for over a year. In 1305, Trúc Lâm gave him ordination as a bhikkhu and as a bodhisattva. In 1306, he was appointed a dharma lecturer at Siêu Loại Pagoda. The first ancestor himself taught Pháp Loa from historical Buddhist books such as Truyền Đăng Lục I (Record of Transmission of the Lamp) and Đại Tuệ Ngữ Lục (The Great Insight Dharma Sentences).[43]

5.8. Monastic Disciples and Lineage of the Trúc Lâm Zen School

Besides Pháp Loa, the Trúc Lâm's second successor, the Patriach Trúc Lâm, also had other monastic disciples such as Bảo Sát, Bảo Phác, Pháp Không, Pháp Cổ và Huệ Nghiêm. In addition, according to the chart of Huệ Nghiêm in the book, Tuệ Trung Thượng Sĩ Ngữ Lục, among Trúc Lâm's disciples were Pháp Tràng, Hương Tràng, Hương Sơn, and Mật Tạng.

5.9. Lineage of Trúc Lâm Zen School

Zen Buddhism has been up and down following the fate of the country, however, according to the book, Lý-Trần Dynasty's Literature (Thơ Văn Lý Trần),[44] the Trúc Lâm Zen School has a long list of successors' transmission of the Zen lamp genre and

---

43 Ibid.
44 Thơ Văn Lý Trần. Nguyễn Huệ Chi. NXB Khoa Học Xã Hội. Hà Nội 1988. File DPF.

upspring in the twentieth and twenty-first century as below:

1. Zen Master Trần Nhân Tông aka Hương Vân đại đầu đà (1258–1308)

2. Zen Master Pháp Loa (1284–1330)

3. Zen Master Huyền Quang (1254–1334)

4. Zen Master An Tâm

5. Zen Master Phù Vân Tĩnh Lự

6. Zen Master Vô Trước

7. Zen Master Quốc Nhất

8. Zen Master Viên Minh

9. Zen Master Đạo Huệ

10. Zen Master Viên Ngộ

11. Zen Master Tổng Trì

12. Zen Master Khuê Sâm

13. Zen Master Sơn Đăng

14. Zen Master Hương Sơn

15. Zen Master Trí Dung

16. Zen Master Huệ Quang

17. Zen Master Chân Trụ

18. Zen Master Vô Phiền . . .

19. Zen Master Thanh Từ (twentieth-twenty-first centuries) . . .

5.10. Works of King Trần Nhân Tông

As the Trúc Lâm Zen master who realized enlightenment and as the king who loved his countries, King Trần Nhân Tông was pained when the foreign invaders came to attack Đại Việt. He wrote many edicts, prose, and poems to express his heart and feeling for the country and Buddhism as below:

• Thiền lâm thiết chủy ngữ lục (Zen Sentences)

• Tăng già toái sự (The Daily Troubles of Monastics)

- Thạch thất my ngữ (Wrong Speech in a Stone House) was copied by King Trần Anh Tông into the Tripitaka for circulation
- Đại hương hải ấn thi tập (The Book of Poetry Imprints of the Great Sea of Fragrant Water)
- Trần Nhân Tông thi tập (Trần Nhân Tông's Poetry Collection)

Trung Hưng thực lục (2 volumes) Recording the Invasion of Yuan Invaders

According to the assessment in Lý Trần's poetry and literature book (volume 2) compiled by Nguyễn Huệ Chi, Trần Thị Băng Thanh, Đỗ Văn Hỷ và Trần Tú Châu, Trần Nhân Tông's poetry has the nature of "a smooth combination of philosophical and worldly sensibility, optimism, love of life, the altruistic heart of a great personality and delicate vibrations, the freedom-loving of an artist"[45] For example:

The country two times faced the invaders as the horse stained the mud

The river of country is stable for thousands of years.

(Xã tắc hai phen chồn ngựa đá

Non sông nghìn thuở vững âu vàng).[46]

Living amid Dust and Enjoying the Way

Living amid dust and enjoying the way,

you should let all things take their course.

When hungry, just eat; when tired, just sleep.

The treasure is in your house; don't search any more.

Face the scenes, and have no thoughts;

---

45 https://vietbooks.info/threads/tho-van-ly-tran-tap-2-quyen-thuong-nxb-khoa-hoc-xa-hoi-1988-nguyen-hue-chi-965-trang.1740/
46 https://zingnews.vn/9-cau-noi-luu-danh-muon-doi-cua-de-vuong-danh-than-nuoc-viet-post873836.html

then you don't need to ask for Zen.

Vietnamese: Cư trần lạc đạo phú

Ở đời vui đạo hãy tùy duyên,
Đói cứ ăn đi mệt ngủ liền.
Có báu trong nhà thôi tìm kiếm,
Vô tâm đối cảnh hỏi chi thiền.
(Translated into Vietnamese: Lê Mạnh Thát)[47]

Confined in a breath, human life is short;
larger than two oceans of gold,
human greed is vast;
while being jailed in the palace of evil,
human suffers.
Blissful incomparably are those who enter the Buddha land.
Vietnamese:
Số đời một hơi thở
Lòng người hai biển vàng
Cung ma dồn quá lắm
Cõi Phật vui nào hơn.
(Translated into Vietnamese: Ven. Thích Thanh Từ) [48]

---

47   Toàn tập Trần Nhân Tông (Whole set on Trần Nhân Tông) Lê Mạnh Thát (In lần thứ 3 có sửa chữa bổ sung). Viện Nghiên Cứu Phật Học Việt Nam. NXB Phương Đông. 1999.
48   Trần Nhân Tông - Đức Vua Sáng Tổ Một Dòng Thiền (Trần Nhân Tông, The King Who Founded A Zen School). Translated and Commented by Nguyen Giac.
https://thuvienhoasen.org/a11751/tran-nhan-tong-duc-vua-sang-to-mot-dong-thien-nguyen-giac

Trần Nhân Tông's Shrine at Huế.

Leisure Time

I live in a serene place,

and see the mind liberated.

The cool wind is seeping

through the shade of cypress trees.

Sitting on a Zen bed beneath a tree,

I read a sutra.

The two words "leisure time" are

more precious than ten thousand gold bars.

Vietnamese:

Cảnh vắng sống yên tự tại hồn,

Bóng tùng gió mát thổi từng cơn.

Giường thiền một quyển kinh bên gốc,

Hai chữ thanh nhàn vạn nén hơn.

(Translated into Vietnamese: Prof. Lê Mạnh Thát) [49]

---

49   Ibid.

King Trần Nhân Tông was a typical poet of the Trần Dynasty. His poetry has a special charm, not only of his lofty and profound ideas, but also because of the beauty that reaches the subtlety of words and expressions. He was considered a typical poet and cultural writer of Đại Việt in the medieval period. His name "Trần Nhân Tông" and "Trúc Lâm Thiền Sư" was given to many schools, associations, streets, cities, and provinces in Vietnam to remember the outstanding Zen Master and compassionate king.

The film, "Phật Hoàng Trần Nhân Tông" (Golden Buddha King Trần Nhân Tông) General director, meritorious artist Văn Lượng and his colleagues from Hải Phòng Television Studio (HFS) have begun pre-production of the forty-five-episode epic drama series, Phật Hoàng Trần Nhân Tông King.

With the enthusiasm of the production units and the contributions of cultural and historical researchers, it is hoped that the film, The Golden Buddha Trần Nhân Tông, will be "an artistic work worthy of the stature of a prominent character in the history of the nation and the world." [50]

5.11. Death and Legacy

In 1307, when Pháp Loa was only twenty-four years old, Trúc Lâm wrote the mind verse and took the medicine bowl to pass on

---

50 https://nhandan.vn/bo-phim-su-thi-phat-hoang-tran-nhan-tong-post387865.html

to Pháp Loa. On the first day of the Lunar New Year (1308), Trúc Lâm passed away. Trúc Lâm officially commissioned Pháp Loa to succeed the abbot of Siêu Loại Pagoda, the second ancestor of Trúc Lâm Buddhism. This happened in the witness of King Anh Tông.

Zen History narrated the moment the Trúc Lâm Master felt free entering the death state as below:

In the eighteenth day of the month, he walked to Tú Lâm Temple at An Kỳ Sanh Mountain. Feeling a headache, he said to two monks in the temple, "I want to hike to Ngọa Vân Peak, but my legs feel weak. What should I do?"

The two monks replied that they would help to carry him up. Coming to Ngọa Vân Temple at the peak, he said thanks to the two monks, and urged them, "Go down the mountain and practice hard; don't play down the matter of birth and death."

In the nineteenth day of the month, he asked his attendant Pháp Không to go to Tử Tiêu Temple at Yên Tử Mountain and tell Bảo Sát to come down and see him urgently.

In the twenty-first day of the month, Bảo Sát arrived at Ngọa Vân Temple.

Trúc Lâm Master saw him and said, "I am departing now. Why do you come so late? If you still are unclear about Buddhist teachings, just ask me now."

Bảo Sát said, "When Mã Tổ felt ill, the head monk asked, 'Dear Master, how do you feel these days?' Mã Tổ replied, 'Sun Face Buddha, Moon Face Buddha.' What did that mean?"

Trúc Lâm Master spoke loudly, "The Three Sovereigns and Five Emperors-what were they?"

(A note should be made here. Sun Face Buddha and Moon Face Buddha are the names of two Buddhas whose faces look like a sun and a moon respectively. Both names are listed in the Ten Thousand Buddhas Sutra. It is said that Sun Face Buddha's life lasted 1,800 years, and Moon Face Buddha's life only one day and one night.)

Bảo Sát asked again, "What does the old saying 'As flowers bloom, so does the silk brocade; as bamboos in the south grow, so do the trees in the north' mean?"

Trúc Lâm Master replied, "They made you blind."

Bảo Sát stopped asking.

Then the sky was dark and gloomy for several days. The birds and monkeys in the forest cried sorrowfully.

In the night of the first day of the eleventh month of that year, the sky became clear and full of shining stars. Trúc Lâm Master asked Bảo Sát, "What time is it now?"

Bảo Sát replied, "The hour of the mouse."

Trúc Lâm Master lifted the curtain, looked out and said, "Now is the time I have to go."

Bảo Sát asked, "Where are you going to?"

Trúc Lâm Master read the poem below.

If you constantly see that all things

are unborn and that all things

are undying, all Buddhas appear

constantly in front of your eyes.

Nothing is coming or going.

Bảo Sát asked, "How about when it is unborn and undying?"

Trúc Lâm Master patted on Bao Sat's mouth, and said, "Don't talk in your sleep."

This were the last minutes of a remarkable noble and royal character who devoted his life to the cause of the dhamma, country, and the people. After a fifteen-year reign, and Trần Nhân Tông lay down as a lion and passed away peacefully at the age of fifty-one, in the year 1308. Trúc Lâm Master lived only half a century; however, the Zen school he founded has become now the largest one in Vietnam, specially with the support of the Great Zen Master Thích Thanh Từ of the twentieth and twenty-first century.

Trần Nhân Tông lay down on his right side as the Mahanirvana Buddha

When Trần Nhân Tông passed away, the court and the people mourned and resounded throughout the world. One historian commented, "There are few kings in the nation's history that are fully recorded about the admiration of the people after their death..."[51]

Pháp Loa obeyed his master's will, performed the cremation ceremony, and collected pieces of five-color bony relics. King Trần Anh Tông built a stupa in the court of Vàm Yên Temple on Yên Tử Mountain. The king named the stupa, "Đại Thánh Trần Triều Trúc

---

51 https://nhandan.vn/bo-phim-su-thi-phat-hoang-tran-nhan-tong-post387865.html

Lâm Đầu Đà Tĩnh Tuệ Giác Hoàng Điều Ngự Tổ Phật." [52]

*One part of Trần Nhân Tông's relics worshipped
at Huệ Quang Stupa*

*The statue of King Giác Hoàng Trần Nhân Tông
in Huệ Quang Stupa*

52   Lê Văn Hưu, Phan Phu Tiên, Ngô Sĩ Liên. 1993. 193.

VI. COMPARISON OF THE GREATNESS BETWEEN KING ASHOKA AND KING TRẦN NHÂN TÔNG

Like Emperor Ashoka, King Trần Nhân Tông traveled all over the country to encourage his people to lead a spiritual life. He also taught ten good deeds for their prosperity.

Now that we have discussed the differences and matters related to the subject, we look into the similarities between the two great emperors.

Both emperors belonged to powerful dynasties from India and Vietnam-Ashoka the Great from the Maurya Dynasty and Emperor King Trần Nhân Tông from the Trần Dynasty.[53]

The reigning period of Dharmassoka was a glorious time of Buddhism in religiously awake India, and in Vietnam as well during the reigning days of King Trần Nhân Tông.

When we go through the life stories of both Ashoka and Trần Nhân Tông, we find both had immense love and affection towards mankind and their fellow living beings and also for Buddhism, despite its sectors or chapters.[54]

The similarity between the two kings is clear when we look into the wars they faced or launched. Emperor Ashoka waged war to expand his kingdom and to create an unchallenged sovereignty. King Trần Nhân Tông waged war to protect his country, citizens, and culture from Mongolian invaders.

However, both had seen the bloodshed with their own eyes and learned lessons. According to historians, millions died as a result of those wars while property in some areas was fully destroyed. Both kings devoted their royal power to spread Buddhism and to perform beneficial activities among Maha Sangha and their beloved subjects.

It is said that King Trần Nhân Tông did not consume fish or meat. Emperor Ashoka, in this regard, proceeding further,

53   Lê Văn Hưu, Phan Phu Tiên, Ngô Sĩ Liên. 1993. 192.
54   Ibid.

prohibited slaughter of animals all over the country. On the other hand, according to their lifestyles, both were brave and had enough courage to face and handle any situation. They both worked with no limit to serve the people for the betterment of their lives.

It seems both may have faced challenges when they were propagating Buddhism as there were other people following different traditional beliefs. When Emperor Ashoka made Buddhism a world religion, Emperor Trần Nhân Tông made the Trúc Lâm Zen sector of Buddhism strong and powerful in his empire.

VII. THE GREAT CONTRIBUTION FOR WORLD PEACE AND SOCIAL HARMONY

Both Emperor Ashoka of India and Emperor Trần Nhân Tông of Vietnam made great contributions for world peace and social harmony for their countries and human beings.

From a murderous and ferocious king, Ashoka became awakened as he saw the bloody river from his conquest of Kalinga on the east coast. Since then, he became an honest gentle follower of the Buddha whose dharma advocates compassion, wisdom and especially non-violence, not injuring others physically or mentally.

Looking at the history of Buddhism is the seeing the history of altruism, sacrifice, care for people, helping people to overcome suffering, live peacefully and happily in the present and future. Therefore, the king used the dharma of the Blessed One to rule the country such as:

7.1. Ten precepts:

- Not to kill or encourage others to kill.

- Not to steal or encourage others to steal.

- Not to engage in licentious acts or encourage others to do so. A monk is expected to abstain from sexual conduct entirely.

- Not to use false words and speech or encourage others to

do so.

- Not to trade or sell alcoholic beverages or encourage others to do so.
- Not to broadcast the misdeeds or faults of the Buddhist assembly, nor encourage others to do so.
- Not to praise oneself and speak ill of others or encourage others to do so.
- Not to be stingy or encourage others to do so.
- Not to harbor anger or encourage others to be angry.
- Not to speak ill of the Buddha, the dharma or the sangha (lit. the Triple Jewel) or encourage others to do so.

Citizens and Buddhists keep the precepts to avoid bad cause-effects and to increase good deeds, providing a safe and happy environment for the individual, family and community.

7.2. Six Harmonious Disciplines

- Harmony in having the same viewpoints
- Hrmony in observing the same precepts
- Harmony in living together
- Harmony in speaking without conflict
- Harmony in experiencing Dharma bliss
- Harmony in sharing benefits.

The six ways of harmony help to connect individuals as a whole who can co-live, co-work, co-share and co-progress on the spiritual path. The country is strong thanks to the harmony of each person, each family, and community. The Ten Precepts and the Six Harmonious Disciplines are a good force for world peace and social harmony.

King Ashoka had these teachings engraved on stone pillars as a decree of maintaining harmony and peace. He ordered the Buddhist missions to bring these happy and liberated messages outside the Indian border, to Ceylon, Thailand, Laos, China,

Vietnam and so on. For example, the king sent his son, the crown prince aka Bhikkhu Mahinda (Mahendra) to Ceylon to establish Buddhism and later he sent his daughter, the Princess Sanghamitra to go Ceylon to ordain nuns and spread the right way to liberation.

In addition, King Asoka was a benefactor who supported the very large sangha by providing financial and food support regularly. To keep the pure sangha, any monk who pretended to infiltrate the sangha, who does not really practice will be severely punished. King Asoka also played the role of a powerful protector who strengthened Buddhism. The king also built many pagodas and erected towers in many states of ancient India.Today the archaeological foundations are still eloquently presented.

Ashoka was the king who was first credited with spreading the Buddha's message of nonviolence, compassion, and wisdom out of India. Buddhism is a way of living peacefully, happily, mindfully and awake. This method has the ability to reforce the transformation of society into an orderly, safe, just, peaceful and happy place. This method has been accepted, existed, and integrated in many countries regardless of the national origin, marital status, ethnicity, color, gender, race, age and occupation. Buddhism can be vividly in harmony with other cultures, religions, philosophies, and organizations to jointly reinforce a liberated world worth living.

As with Emperor Asoka, King Trần Nhân Tông took the Ten Precepts, Six Hamonious Disciplines and studied the Zen philosophy of Buddhism as the main thought to build the Buddhist-based society. He led his citizens and Buddhist disciples to cultivate wisdom and virtue, unite people's hearts, protect the country from foreign invaders, and build a peaceful state.

When the country was unsafe by aggression, King Trần Nhân Tông put aside his spiritual practice to defend his country to protect the state. He governed the country keeping the people safe, and expressed the spirit of national self-reliance, which will be remembered forever.

When the country was at peace, he focused on education, selection of a Mandarin system, building a state apparatus with integrity, so that the society would be just, equal, and developed. When his son was mature enough to run the kingdom, he yielded the throne to him and become a monk who lived a simple and ascetic life to search for the truth on a remote mountain. He became enlightened and shared the way of awakening (the Trúc Lâm Zen School) to all which are still well illustrated by his poems, edicts, and works in the Trần Dynasty.

With the wisdom and profound vision of a Zen Master, he understood that Buddhist teachings are the place to relieve suffering and save lives, help sentient beings give up evil, do good and live purely. Being a king must be ethical for the sake of sentient beings. He built a good model to bring harmony in the sangha, royalty, and society for his citizens and Buddhist disciples. He applied the practice of the six Buddhist Harmonious Rules to build a peaceful and prosperous Đại Việt country.

Firstly, in terms of diplomacy, he attempted to build a close friendship with the neighboring country located on the southern border, Champa. To tighten the diplomatic relationship that had good momentum, to discourage the Đại Việt people from the looting of their Champa neighbors and increase the peacekeeping, King Trần Nhân Tông sent his daughter, Princess Huyền Trân, to Champa to marry King Che Man. In regard to the wedding betrothal of the bride, King Chế Mân offered the two provinces of Châu Ô and Châu Lý (the present is Thuận Châu and Hóa Châu of Vietnam)[55.] Ever since, both countries have been friends with a connection. This peace and harmony extended to the surrounding areas.

Secondly, in order to consolidate the long-term peace, he released prisoners of the Mongolian-Yuan that the army captured in the three wars to create favorable conditions for relations between the two countries, a wise and flexible decision in Đại Việt's foreign policy at that time. Perhaps that is why Trần Nhân Tông is considered by the world as the most representative of the spirit of social reconciliation and world peace.

---

55   https://sdl.thuathienhue.gov.vn/?gd=20&cn=1&id=232&tc=4165

VIII. CONLCUSION

In the history of the nation and Buddhim, Ashoka and Trần Nhân Tông were outstanding emperors in India and Vietnam. They advocated bringing Buddhism into the world, actively spreading it among the people, promoting the spirit of harmony among hundreds of families, building and fostering independence, self-reliance, and harmony in the world, harmony between king-prince, harmony between father-son, harmony between husband-wife, family, and the nation. That thought is the root of the nation's lasting strength, and over time has become a tradition of the nation. They created a civilized and good Buddhist-based society for themselves and for the global community. Indeed, Emperor Ashoka and King Trần Nhân Tông were keepers of world peace and social harmony.

The lives of both emperors are an invaluable legacy for posterity. They have become international figures who are the source of inspiration for future generations.

Kolkata, July 2, 2023

Ven. Dr. Bhikṣuṇī TN Gioi Huong

huongsentemple@gmail.com

SOURCES

- Aher, D.C. Ashoka the Great. Delhi: B.R. Publishing Corporation, 1995.

- Ayyar, Sulochana. Costumes and Ornaments as Depicted in the Early Sculptures of Gwarlior Museum. Mittal Publications: South Asia Books, 1987.

- Bandarkar, B.R. Ashoka. Kolkata: Calcutta University, 1999.

- Bapat, Professor P.V. ed. 2500 Years of Buddhism. India: Department of Information, Government of India, 1959.

- Bhandarakar, D.R. Aśoka. Calcutta: Calcutta University Press, 1969.

- Bongard-Levin, G.M. Mauryan India. Stosius, 1986.

- Chand, S. Kalinga Rock Edicts–Ancient India. New Delhi: S. Chand and Co. Ltd. Publishers, 2008.

- Chauhan, Giand Chand. Origin and Growth of Feudalism in Early India: From the Mauryas to AD 650. Delhi: Munshiram Manoharlal Publishers, 2004

- Đại Việt Sử Ký Toàn Thư (National Bureau for Historical Record). Lê Văn Huru, Phan Phu Tiên, Ngô Sĩ Liên. Viện Khoa Học Xã Hội Việt Nam dịch (1985–1992).

- https://www.tuvienquangduc.com.au/lichsu/lichsuvietnam/Daivietsukytoanthu.pdf

- Dharmapala, Ven. Maha Thera. Ashoka. India, Kolkata: The Bengal Buddhist Association, 1997.

- Gokhale, Balkrishna Govind. Ashoka Maurya. New York: Twayne Publishers, Inc., 1966.

- Hạnh, Ven. Thích Nhất, Việt Nam Phật giáo Sử luận (History of Vietnamese Buddhism), tập 1,2,3. Nguyễn Lang, Lá Bối. 1973. https://langmai.org/tang-kinh-cac/vien-sach/giang- kinh/viet-nam-phat-giao-su-luan/chuong-12-tran-nhan-tong-va-thien-phai-truc-lam/

- Hazra, Kanai Lal. Royal Patronage of Buddhism in Ancient India. New Delhi (India): D.K. Publications, 1984.

- Kiskalar, D.B. "Literary Value of Inscriptions of Ashoka," Journal of Indian History. New Delhi. Mahajan, V.D. Ancient India. New Delhi: S. Chand Publishing, 2016.

- Malasekera, Dr. G.P. ed. Encyclopaedia of Buddhism, Vol. II. Sri Lanka: Government of Ceylon, Colombo, 1967.

- Medhankara, Ven. Dr. Maha Thero. The Great Buddhist Emperors of Asia. Maharashrata, India: Bhoomi Prakashan. Nagpur, 1959.

- Nikam, N.A. and McKeon, Richard, eds. The Edicts of Ashoka. Chicago: University of Chicago Press, 1978.

- Smith, Vincent A. Asoka and the Buddhist Emperors of India. Delhi: Low Price Publications, 1930.

- Thích Hạnh Thành. Biên Niên Sử Thiền Tông Việt Nam (1010–2000).

- Toàn tập Trần Nhân Tông (Whole Set on Trần Nhân Tông) Lê Mạnh Thát, 3rd ed. Viện Nghiên Cứu Phật Học Việt Nam. NXB Phương Đông. 1999.

- Trần Nhân Tông - Đức Vua Sáng Tổ Một Dòng Thiền (Trần Nhân Tông, The King Who Founded a Zen School). Translation and Commentary by Nguyen Giac.

- https://thuvienhoasen.org/a11751/tran-nhan-tong-duc-vua-sang-to-mot-dong-thien-nguyen-giac

- Thích Thanh Từ. Vietnamese Zen in the Late Twentieth Century. https://thientruclam.info/ht-thich-thanh-tu/thien-tong-viet-nam-cuoi-the-ky-20. NXB Hồng Đức. 2016.

- https://hoavouu.com/a48178/bien-nien-su-thien-tong-viet-nam-1010-2000

- Thơ Văn Lý Trần. Nguyễn Huệ Chi. NXB Khoa Học Xã Hội. Hà Nội 1988.

- Thiền Uyển Tập Anh. Dịch giả Nguyễn Huệ Chi. Phân viện Nghiên cứu Phật Học.NXB Văn Học. Hà Nội 1990.

- http://thuongchieu.net/index.php/phapthoai/suong/1960-pht-giao-thin-tong-vit-nam

BUDDHIST CONTRIBUTIONS FOR WORLD PEACE

Dr. Siddharth M. Jondhale

MD, PhD, DSc, DLit

Director of Siddharth Research Centre

Winner of the Albert Schweitzer Award, 2011

Abstract

The omniscience of the Buddha offers peace and scientific Abhidhamma for the revolution of the world. Understanding of the great work of the Abhidhamma (Buddhist metaphysical science) is crucial to understanding the nature of reality. Peace is a concept of societal friendship and harmony with the absence of hostility and violence. In a social sense, peace is commonly used to mean a lack of conflict (such as war) and freedom from fear of violence between individuals or groups.

The Buddhist way of peace is understanding, accepting, adaptation of *kenāchidhammā, tisso vijjya, abāyaktādhammā, sōtapanna, sakadāgāmi, anāgāmi, arahatta,* and *arammaṇapaccayo* (object condition), *aññamaññapaccayo* (mutuality condition), *adhipatipaccayā* (dominant causes) for the creation of peace for humanity and for world peace.

Buddhist epistemology, Buddhist cosmology, and Buddhist metaphysical science result in Buddhist peace. The omniscience of the Buddha can create a spiritual revolution in the world. The Abhidhamma teaches twenty-four conditional relations (*paccaya*) and provides an examination of causal conditioning which include evolution, expression, and spiritual divine power (*pariyatti*), the infinite cosmic world (nature), the path (*pātipada*), and attainment of entrance onto the path (*paṭivedha*). The Tathāgata says the mind is very important for enlightenment. It contains the inherent nature of a human being.

The Abhidhamma is inherent and reveals an infinite dynamic in nature. It describes the eternal relationship of the human mind on a cosmological level, consciousness level, and physical level. The omniscience of the Buddha is contained in the *pariyātidhammā, paṭipadādhammā,* and *paṭivedhadhammā*. The Buddha offered ultimate teachings on the nature of mind and reality, a metaphysical science for a revolution of world peace and wisdom and for the world's benefit.

Omniscience of the Buddha with Buddhist Contributions for World Peace

The *pariyātidhammā, paṭipadādhammā, paṭivedhadhammā* with *ārammaṇapaccayo* (conditional relationship) and Buddhist metaphysical science belong to the infinity cosmology that is interrelated with conditional relationships and Abhidhamma, which represent the peace and omniscience of the Buddha. This is the correlation of omniscience of the Buddha for world peace and Buddhist scientific social revolution for health, treating diseases, and daily life.

Abhidhamma metaphysical science has interrelationships for feeling and daily life. The mind is important to the feeling (*vedanā*); all feeling that arises in the mind can be expressed in ways of consciousness. Abhidhamma feeling of the cosmic way has eternal connections to dependent origination. Therefore, *vedanā* expresses the nature which belongs to the infinite cosmology. *Kusalādhammā* is for practice in daily life. *Kusalādhammā* are natural qualities of the human mind that represent peace.

Considerations from the Abhidhamma: A *sotāpanna* (stream-enterer) is the nature of a human being which can develop the great spiritual qualities within the mind which are representations of peace. Considerations from the Abhidhamma are the representations of peace-infinite metaphysical cosmology representations of nature and peace.

Infinite spiritual metaphysical consciousness: the first moment of the attainment is termed "entering the path." The person who experiences it is called a stream-winner *(sotāpanna)*. This metaphor is a representation of peace-the infinite spiritual metaphysical consciousness, infinite understanding and adaptation, application of the five precepts (*pañcasīla, pariyātidhammā, paṭipadādhammā, paṭivedhadhammā*) in daily life i.e., representations of stream consciousness and representations of peace. *Hetupaccayo* (root condition) from which *ārammaṇapaccayo (*object condition*)* arises are representations of the infinite Buddhist cosmology, as well as nature.

The Abhidhamma cosmology reflects the omniscience of the Buddha-the nature which can be analyzed through rebirth consciousness. Abhidhamma, dynamic conditional relations, and dependent origination in Buddhist infinite conditional relations are dynamic in nature and reflect the omniscience of the Buddha.

Correlations of the Omniscience of the Buddha and Meditation

For peace and happiness, daily practice of mindfulness breathing is the great and scientific principle for the benefit of the world. Understanding the great Buddhist metaphysical science is important to humanity for the evolution of world peace.

Methods of Adaptation for Daily Peace

Daily deep reflection on the holistic way of the scientific Buddhist word, *kenāchidhammā*, belongs to the daily formation of peace inside the mind.

Practicing kindness is an *adhipatipaccaya* (dominant cause). Kindness belongs to the eradication of anger, hostility, and jealousy which can be transformed to peace in a human being by using the methods of practice of the Buddhist scientific social revolution.

Meditation of mindfulness breathing, holistic natural energy for daily practice, *kenāchidhammā, sōtapanna, sakadāgāmi, anāgāmi, arahatt, ārammaṇapaccayo* (object condition), *aññamaññapaccayo* (mutuality condition), and *adhipatipaccaya* (dominant cause).

Buddha said thinking with mindfulness belongs to the formation of a new creation of thought for peace, health, and for the universe as well-for *Nibbāna bhumi*. This is the mechanism of the mind and body. Thinking with mindfulness, breathing with creation of the natural energy of *kenāchidhammā,* thoughts for a new creation of peace in the mind, a Buddhist habit for natural daily energy.

Conclusion

The omniscience of the Buddha shows the correlation between world peace and Buddhist scientific social revolution. Peace is a concept of societal friendship and harmony in the absence of hostility and violence. In a social sense, peace is commonly used to mean a lack of conflict (such as war) and freedom from fear of violence between individuals or groups. Understanding, accepting, adaptating *kenāchidhammā sōtapanna, sakadāgāmi, anāgāmi, arahatta and ārammaṇapaccayo* (object condition), *aññamaññapaccayo* (mutuality condition), *adhipatipaccaya* (dominant causes) for the creation of peace for humanity.

Gratitude

My Dear Great Brother, Ven. Dr. Buddha Priya Mahathero,

gratitude for your blessing, love, and compassion for me and for my Abhidhamma research work.

REFERENCES

- The Pali Tripitaka
- Wikipedia, *The Free Encyclopedia.* https://en.wikipedia.org/w/index.php?title=Peace&oldid=1169512135

BUDDHISM AND BENGALIS: SIDDHARTH UNITED SOCIAL WELFARE MISSION AND ITS FOUNDER

Dr. Palash Bandyopadhyay
Physician, Writer, Kolkata, India

*B*uddhism is not a religion per se, instead, it's a philosophy in a broader sense-a philosophy of peace, love, and universal brotherhood. Peace is defined and explained in so many ways. In a deeper sense, it signifies happiness and harmony among living creatures. Being peaceful is living in harmony with self as well as others. Peace, like energy, is not visible but its existence is felt by the mind and threatened by violence, distrust, hostility, bloodshed, and war. Buddhists explain peace as an inner state of mental tranquility which spreads outwards. Understanding peace as absence of violence is merely a narrow vision. To achieve a mental state of inner peace could be and must be an ultimate aim for every human being.

As per Buddhist philosophy, inner peace can only be secured by practicing meditation, which ultimately is an inspiration for a world free of war.

In most of his teachings, Lord Buddha stressed the practice of vipassana which uproots mental defilements, which are, as per his vision, the cause of sufferings and mental restlessness. Once suffering has been overcome, the mental state of inner peace is felt. Inner peace has a unique feature of projecting itself outwards towards family, friends, and the larger society, ensuring peace and harmony in the outer world.

Now, before further discussion, let me discuss the Four Noble Truths and the Noble Eightfold Path, the practice which is the ultimate way of Nirvana, that is, a transcendent state in which there is neither suffering, desire, nor sense of self, and the subject is released from the effects of karma and the cycle of death and rebirth. It represents the final goal of Buddhism.

Before discussing further Buddhism and world peace, let me discuss the basics of Buddhist philosophy, which are the Four Noble Truths realized by the Buddha while seated in contemplation under the Bodhi tree at Bodh Gaya were made known by him to his erstwhile companions, the five ascetics, when he gave his first sermon at the Deer Park at Isipatana (modern Sarnath) near Benaras. These are *dukkha* (suffering), *samudaya* (the arising of suffering), *nirodha* (the cessation of suffering), and *magga* (the path leading to cessation of suffering).

The magga or path is further subdivided into eight sections which are popularly known as *astangik marg*. They are right understanding, right thought, right speech, right action, right livelihood, right effort, right mindfulness, and right concentration.

In India, Buddhism was an outstanding representation of our living tradition, that is, peace and harmony. Humanism, which was the essence of the Buddha's teaching, crossed all racial and national barriers. But unfortunately today, the scenario is different. Now we are suffering from an exhaustion of spirit, an increase of egoism, individual and collective, which makes the ideal of a world society difficult to achieve.

The Buddha's policy of peace, self-sacrifice, kindness, and charity imaged the lives of numerous saints in medieval India and modern India too. The declared foreign policy of India was based on *panchashila*, a Buddhist term that allows the possibility of peaceful co-existence between people of different ideologies. Buddhism has an intimate association with peace. It wields only one sword, the sword of wisdom and recognizes only one enemy and that is ignorance.

The message of Buddhism and the principles on which it rests (*maitri*) have assumed a new significance in the present time. Even the peace that UNO speaks of is but an indication that the world is gradually approaching belief in the concept of Buddhism.

Though world peace today appears to be a myth, a mirage, yet despite the diversity of race, religion, ideology and so on, common people of whole world are in a continuous seeking for peace and happiness. International humanitarianism, nonviolence, and world peace are a dire need of today's world. The problem of peace, whether of an individual or the masses, is basically a problem of mind. It's the positive state of the human mind, which is the forerunner of peace.

A majority of the world of today is the living space of anarchists and violence makers. In this context, Buddhism lifts not only their community, but also the entire human race above and beyond the ignorance, fear, and isolation which are the causative factors of instability of the entire world. The Buddha realized that a peaceful world is possible only when the mankind is happy and without tension. If humans get rid of all malice, hatred, indulgence in lower desires and evil thoughts and purify their thoughts and desires with complete happiness then the world would be peaceful again.

Buddhism, in this way, elevates the humanistic tendency in mankind with the help of morality, karuna, and samata. In the changing world of today, Buddhism has a great deal to contribute to establishing peace by way of the concept of commonwealth of Dharma.

In some early Buddhist scriptures and later Mahayana philosophical and literary works, there are certain specific references to peace. Earlier works like the Kimsita Sutra of Cullavagta firmly state the association between meditation, knowledge, and peace.

The three sutras of Mahavagga, most of the sutras of Atthaka Vagga, and the complete chapter of Parayanavagga support the Buddhist's conception of peace as one's individual attainment of complete mental freedom. The concept of the peace of Buddhism is also reflected in two important Buddhist works, Saddharmapundarika Sutra or Lotus of the True Law, and the Kalachakra Tantra or the Wheel of Time.

History of Buddhism in India

The historical background that caused the rise of Buddhism in the sixth century BC was the result of the development of the force of production in the northern region of India, which witnessed the rise of ruthless state powers on the ruins of tribal societies.

Buddhism is an ancient Indian religion that arose in and around the ancient Kingdom of Magadha (now in Bihar, India), and is based on the teachings of Lord Buddha who was deemed a "Buddha" although Buddhist doctrine holds that there were other Buddhas before him. Buddhism spread outside of Magadha starting in the Buddha's lifetime.

The Great Stupa at Sanchi, located in Sanchi, Madhya Pradesh, is a Buddhist shrine in India. The Mahabodhi Temple, a UNESCO World Heritage Site, is one of the four holy sites related to the life of the Lord Buddha, and particularly to the attainment of enlightenment. The first temple was built by the Indian Emperor Ashoka in the third century BC, and the present temple dates from the fifth or sixth century AD. It is one of the earliest Buddhist temples built entirely in brick still standing in India from the late Gupta period.

During the reign of the Mauryan Emperor, Ashoka the Great, the Buddhist community split into two branches: the Mahāsāṃghika and the Sthaviravāda, each of which spread throughout India and split into numerous subsects. In modern times, two major branches of Buddhism exist: the Theravada in Sri Lanka and Southeast Asia, and the Mahayana throughout the Himalayas and East Asia. The Buddhist tradition of Vajrayana is sometimes classified as a part of Mahayana Buddhism, but some scholars consider it to be a different branch altogether.

The practice of Buddhism lost influence in India around the seventh century CE, after the collapse of the Gupta Empire. The causes of the decreasing influence of Buddhism are corruption in the Buddhist Sangha, division among Buddhists, use of Sanskrit language, Buddha worship, persecution of Buddhists, Muslim invasion, and revival and reform of Vedic Brahmanism.

The last large state to support Buddhism, the Pala Empire, fell in the twelfth century. By the end of the twelfth century, Buddhism had largely disappeared from India with the exception of the Himalayan region and isolated remnants in parts of south India. However, since the nineteenth century, modern revivals of Buddhism have included the Maha Bodhi Society, the Vipassana movement, and the Dalit Buddhist movement spearheaded by B. R. Ambedkar. There has also been a growth in Tibetan Buddhism with the arrival of the Tibetan diaspora and the Tibetan government in exile in India, following the Chinese annexation of Tibet in 1950. According to the 2011 Census there are 8.4 million Buddhists in India (0.70 percent of the total population).

Bengali Buddhists

Bengali Buddhists are a religious subgroup of the Bengalis who adhere to or practice the religion of Buddhism. Bengali Buddhist people mainly live in Bangladesh and the Indian states of West Bengal and Tripura.

Total populations:

Bangladesh 350,000

India 408,080 (West Bengal (282,898) and Tripura (125,182)

Languages are Bengali (native), Sanskrit and Pali (liturgical), English and Hindi. Their subtype is Theravada.

Buddhism has a rich ancient heritage in Bengal. The region was a bastion of the ancient Buddhist Mauryan and Palan empires when the Mahayana and Vajrayana schools flourished. Southeastern Bengal was ruled by the medieval Buddhist Kingdom of Mrauk U during the sixteenth and seventeenth centuries. The British Raj influenced the emergence of the modern community.

Today, Bengali Buddhists are followers of the Theravada tradition.

Siddharth United Social Welfare Mission, Buddha Priya Mahathero, and Buddhism in West Bengal

SUSWM is an organization of international repute for rendering humanitarian services. Siddharth United Social Welfare Mission is dedicated to the noble cause of supporting those children who are deprived of the fundamental rights in life. There are three centers run by the organization simultaneously in three parts of India with headquarters in Chinar Park, Kolkata. The mission is to provide yeomen services to the destitute, tribal children, and needy students by providing education, shelter, nutrition, health care, meditation instruction, and other services.

Ven. Buddha Priya Mahathero is the founder of the organization He is doing a great service to combine the spirit of compassion with humanitarian service. Ven. Buddha Priya Mahathero is an exceptional monk, free from all bias and sectarian attitude. He is a very liberal-minded Buddhist with deep respect for all religions. He has a wide circle of admirers all over the world. They are all impressed by the singularly humanitarian service he has been rendering in India, especially in bringing up more than one hundred orphan tribal boys. He and his organization, SUSWM, are taking care of their food, shelter, studies-all their needs. His aim is to serve the poor. It is by serving humanity that he wants everyone's heart to beat for a better world.

REFERENCES

- Ambedkar, B.R. 1996. *Bauddha Dharma O Darshan*. Mahabodhi Book Agency, Kolkata.

- Barua, Rudiak Kumar, *Buddhist Philosophy*. India.

- Barua, Sukomal. 2022. Bharate Bauddha Dharmer Itihas, Bangladesh: Dhaka University.

- https://baruasamaj.com/2022/07/30/bharate-bauddha-dharmer-itihas/

- *Brainwave: A Multidisciplinary Journal*, Vols 1–5.

- Brammachary, Pandit Silananda. 2011. *Mahasanti Mahaprem*. Kolkata: Maha Bodhi Book Agency.

- Das, Asha. 2013. *Bauddha Darshan O Rabindranath*. India: Calcutta University.

- Dev, Acharya Narendra. 2015. *Bauddha Dharma Darshan*. (Hindi) Vols. 1–6. India: Motilal Banarsidass Publishing House.

- Mahasthavir, Pandit Dharmadar. 1994. *Dhammapada*, Dharmadhar Bouddha Grantha Prakasani, Calcutta.

- Sankrityayan, Mahapandita Rahul. 2016. *Buddhist Philosophy* Haoladar Prakasani, Bangladesh.

- Sen, Ranabrata, ed. 1968. *Dhammapada*. Haraf Prakasani, Kolkata.

- Sherab, Khenchen Palden Rinpoche and Dongyal, Khenpo Tsewang Dongyal Rinpoche. 1997. *The Light of Peace,* 2nd ed. New York: Padmasambhava Buddhist Centre, 7, 13, 22.

- Tagore, Rabindranath. 1984. *Maitri Bhavana O Bauddha Darshan*. Shantiniketan, India: Visva Bharati University.

- Vivekananda, Swami. 1998. *Buddha o Bauddha Dharma*. West Bengal, India: Belur Math.

- Wikipedia, The Free Encyclopedia. "2011 Census of

India," https://en.wikipedia.org/w/index.php?title=2011_Census_of_India&oldid=116867815 9 (accessed August 9, 2023).

THE BUDDHA: HIS PERVASIVE HUMANISM

Honorable Justice Arunabha Barua

Former Judge, Calcutta High Court

Namo Tassaa Bhagavato Samma Sambuddhassa

Homage to the Buddha, the Exalted, the Worthy, the Fully Enlightened One!

*O*n the full moon day of May, year 623 BC, there was born in the Lumbini Park at Kapilavatthu on the Indian borders of present-day Nepal, a noble prince who was destined to be the greatest religious teacher of the world. The highly reputed Swami Vivekananda of the famous Ramkrishna Mission Institute of India had truly put it right that the Buddha was the "greatest humanist on Earth."

Truly speaking, "Buddhism" is no doctrine of divine dispensation, no magic moment of windfall from the sky. Buddhism is a learning the lessons of life, serene and sublime. It is essentially divine without any divinity declared. For it, "work is worship," man is the creator of his own fate. It primarily stands for peace, nonviolence with harmony and happiness for humanity at large through intense humanitarian activities. This is the need of the hour today all over the world.

The Buddha's greatness lies in the fact that he proclaimed to the world the latent possibilities and invincible power of the human mind. He showed the way to us for emancipation from the eternal cycle of sorrow and suffering, from decay, disease, and death by attainment of the eternal bliss of "Nibbana" by our own efforts without depending upon an eternal God. The Buddha strenuously propounded the noble ideal of selfless service to humanity.

Our most celebrated, world-famous poet having had the glorious Nobel Prize, among many of his poetic exuberance and excellence has this solemn submission before the Buddha:

> *Buddha, my Lord, my Master,*
>
> *Remove the blackness of all sins,*
>
> *Victory be to thee.*
>
> *Sprinkle the world with water*
>
> *Of everlasting life*
>
> *Thou are the fountain of peace*
>
> *Of welfare, of holiness, of love.*
>
> *(Buddhadeva by Tagore)*

Now, a humanist is one who is, simply, all for the good and welfare for the people, for society and humanity at large without ever the need of orthodox religious rites and rituals, set ideas and beliefs. A humanist is necessarily humane, that is, kind, tolerant, sympathetic as well as empathetic towards his follow human beings, having no conceit, ill will or ego. He is truly dedicated to selfless service to humanity. Humanism propagates, among others, equality, liberty, and fraternity for all in a civilized society, irrespective of their caste, creed, religion, and sex. The Buddha was one of the greatest teachers of humanism, of "Humanistic Buddhism" with His invaluable precepts and practices, and codes of human conduct to follow in our daily life in order to achieve abiding peace, harmony, and happiness.

In this connection, "humanistic Buddhism" predominantly pertains to one excellent element, which is called *metta* in Pali. It means and signifies loving-kindness, generosity, goodwill, benevolence, and the sense of universal love towards all beings on earth, including animals. Thus, the Buddha advises:

Just as a mother protects her only child even

at the risk of her own life, even so

one should cultivate boundless loving-kindness

towards all living beings.

(Piyadassi, 2011)

Together with this, one other great trait of Buddhism is *ahimsa* or *karuna*, that is, harmlessness or compassion. Karuna is that softness of heart which cannot bear the sufferings of others. It certainly motivates us to try our best and help the downtrodden and the distressed, hundreds and thousands of our men, women, and children, suffering in silence being victims of atrocities, cruelty and violence perpetrated by the rich and powerful against the poor, hapless and the hopeless day in and day out. The Buddha has untiringly shown to humanity and the entire world how to attain the cessation of jealousy, hatred and ill-will which leads to mindless violence, terrorism, death, and destruction.

Indeed, we might deeply think that it is our mind that is our best friend and yet the worst enemy. Which is why, in Buddhistic preaching and practices, mindfulness and meditation are the twin imperatives that reign supreme to reach the milestone of eternal bliss-Nibbana.

Sabbe Satta Sukhita Hantu
May All Beings Be Happy

REFERENCES

- Barua, Dipak Kumar. 2015. *Buddhist Philosophy.* Createspace Publishing, California, USA.

- Sherab, Khenchen Palden Rinpoche and Dongyal, Khenpo Tsewang Dongyal Rinpoche. 1997. *The Light of Peace,* 2nd ed. New York: Padmasambhava Buddhist Centre, 7, 13, 22.

- Sherab, Khenchen Palden Rinpoche and Dongyal, Khenpo Tsewang Dongyal Rinpoche. 2019. *The Light of Peace: How Buddhism Shines in the World,* New York: Padmasambhava   Buddhist Centre.

- Mahasthavir, Pandit Dharmadar. 1994. *Dhammapada,* Dharmadhar Bouddha Grantha Prakasani, Calcutta-15.

- Piyadassi, Maha Thera. 2011. *The Book of Protection.* Sri Lanka: Buddhist Publication Society, Inc.

- Sen, Ranabrata, ed. 1968. *Dhammapada,* Haraf Prakasani, Kolkata.

- Tagore, Rabindranath. 1984. *Maitri Bhavana O Bauddha Darshan.* Shantiniketan, India: Visva Bharati University.

- Tagore, Rabindranath. 1934. *Buddhadeva.* India: Shantiniketan Press.

- Vivekananda, Swami. 1996 (8th ed.). *Buddha o Bauddha Dharma.* West Bengal, India: Belur   Math.

CONTRIBUTIONS OF BUDDHISM FOR WORLD PEACE AND SOCIAL HARMONY

Shri Kishore Bhattacharya

Assistant Lecturer, Visva Bharati, Santiniketan 731235, Birbhum, WB, India

$\mathcal{W}$e call Mahatma Gandhi the apostle of peace and nonviolence. The father of the nation, however, was in many ways a successor to the Great Lord Buddha and an inheritor of the great Buddhist tradition. More than 2600 years ago, Lord Buddha taught the whole of mankind the lessons of peace and nonviolence. Indeed, Buddha is the "*adipurush*" of peace, love and nonviolence-an icon of the icons of peace and social harmony. Having arrived at the second half of twenty-first century it is imperative to assess or to re-assess whether the views and ideas of

Buddhism still bear any relevance today.

Renunciation, Emancipation, and Enlightenment

The first thing that strikes us about Buddha is his act of renunciation. To some it is baffling as they think that being the son of a king he could well have enjoyed all the pleasures of the world -the material and the physical pleasures. These people fail to understand that there is no self-illumination without renunciation. The path to enlightenment lies is renunciation. Great Buddha could not have achieved enlightenment by enjoying the pleasures of the world. More importantly, he left the family for the betterment and emancipation of humankind, to understand the deeper mysteries of life. The searching questions why there is old age and disease or why an old man suffers, could not have occurred to him had he immersed himself in the worldly pleasures. In other words, Buddha renounced the world for the emancipation of mankind from pain, suffering, and sorrows. Here Buddha and Buddhism are on the same footing with Jesus Christ and Christianity. Both Buddha and Christ suffered to end the sufferings of the world.

Who Is a Real Buddhist?

Enlightenment, an inner psychological state of peace, knowledge, and wisdom is the key to Buddhism. And so great liberal is the teaching of Buddhism that it emphasizes that one can have enlightenment not by practicing false and run-of-the mill rituals but by practicing morality, meditation, and truthfulness. Anyone, high or low, rich or poor, can have access to "truth" if he leads an honest and truthful life. In a wider sense, all of us are "Buddhists" since all the religious of the world speak of truth and enlightenment as key to mental and social development. Buddhism, in this regard, becomes an all-encompassing world religion as it considers illumination of the self and the society to be of paramount importance. All religions, at their heart, have the concept of the need for inner awakening.

A Nonviolent Religion

Violence has no place in Buddhism. Buddhism stands for

karuna or compassion against cruelty and hatred. This, again, is one of the many noble virtues of Buddhism and also one of the reasons why, in today's world, the teachings of Buddha are so relevant. As already indicated, Buddha championed the cause of peace far ahead of Gandhi. But what are we witnessing in today's world? To quote Tagore, "the world is mad with the dance of violence" (Quayum, 2017). To quote Shakespeare, human beings are "preying upon human beings like monsters of the deep." (King Lear). We find the high and the mighty browbeating the poor and the lowly and imperialist tendencies of big nations trying to gobble up the so-called poor nations. Here, the benign message of nonviolence and peace could act as a soothing balm and eradicate the conflict between the rich and poor, the almighty and the powerless. Taking a cue from Buddhism, we might say that instead of showing power and strength, everyone should show compassion and tolerance.

Humanism

One of the main characteristics of human civilization is humanism that flourished during the European Renaissance. Love for mankind is at the heart of humanism. As the Italian humanist Terence suggested, everything that is human is within the range of my interest. Recognition of the dignity of humans happens to be the heart of Buddhism as well. In this, Buddhists are on the same page with our renowned Bengali poet, Joydev, who wrote that above everything, humans embody the highest truth. Buddhism placed the importance and dignity of humans on such a high pedestal that casteism or untouchability religious bigotry was totally kept outside the purview of the religion of Buddhism. Many great people from down-trodden walks of life, like Ambedkar, embraced Buddhism. In this connection, it would be extremely relevant to refer to the role of the Buddhist monk Ananda in Tagore's "Chandalika," who offered water to the girl coming from the community of untouchables.

Influence on Tagore

Tagore, in fact, was greatly influenced by Buddhism and held Lord Buddha to be one of the greatest emancipators of mankind.

It is not only in the dance-drama "Chandalika" or in "Bisarjan" or "Natir Puja" that the influence of the humanist outlook of Buddhism are visible, but in the poetic works like "Sonar Tari," "Balaka," "Geetimalya," and even in the novel *Rajarshi*, the profound influence of Buddhism is to be discovered. Tagore's songs reverberate with profound influence of Buddhism. You would be delighted to know that Visva Bharati offers course on Buddhist Studies which is yet recognition of the relevance of Buddhism in the modern world.

Relevancy of Buddhism in the Modern World

The Buddha emphasized the Eightfold Path as a means to enlightenment, a necessary raft for crossing a river. The Buddha was acutely aware of the devastating effects of hatred and had seen individuals ruin themselves due to its influence. According to Buddha, hatred never ceases by hatred. Only by one party stopping can it be resolved. Loving-kindness, the cornerstone of Buddhism, is not merely a simple ethical principle but rather an analyzed principle that leads to sublime life. The Buddha also preached *karuna*, compassion, which is quickly generated by our hearts when we see someone in trouble. Lastly, there is total equanimity, *upekkha*, where we have no friends, no enemies, no one higher or lower, and totally merge with all beings, things, and situations. Living a life governed by these four characteristics eliminates hatred, rivalry, and competition.

Another crucial aspect of the Buddha's teachings is bhavana, meditation, which means training of the mind. The Buddha believed that everything emanates from the mind and that a pure, trained, well-developed, controlled, alert, and continuously developing mind is human's greatest treasure. In this scientifically and technologically advanced global village, despite the abundance of amenities for convenience and pleasure, people remain unsatisfied both physically and mentally, lacking a sense of security. True safety is achieved when the mind is free from physical danger, yet this experience is scarce in today's world. Modern life may evoke both optimism and pessimism, as we conquer countless challenges but lose something in the process. However, Buddhism remains relevant in modern life due to its timeless application and set of eternal values.

Conclusion

Buddha's teaching provides many practical techniques that are useful for calming anger, controlling desire, and creating harmonious relationships. The present world is full of violence and corruption. People need comfort that comes from a spiritual path and teaches nonviolence, contentment, compassion, generosity of spirit, and peace of mind. Buddhism teaches us to cultivate peace in our hearts and work to relieve the sufferings of all living beings. Peace at a national, as well as global level, can be possible only if we apply Buddhism in our daily life. The main goals of Buddhism are to secure and maintain peace, happiness, social welfare, and harmony in human society all over the world.

We have to join hands with all in order to raise the world-embracing vision of a Buddha where all nations, injustices, wars, and discrimination will vanish. We have to develop better understanding among peoples with different cultures and cooperate together to improve the lives of the people, not only spiritually and intellectually but also socially and economically in terms of proper utilization of resources available. Buddha's message of peace and compassion is very essential to unite us all in an atmosphere of peace and political stability. Buddhism must address current social problems such as racism, sexism, environmental deterioration, and economic injustice. We must join hands to demonstrate our commitment towards peace by connecting social and economic inequalities.

The present lecture thus shows that the Buddhist ideals of love, peace, enlightenment, tolerance, and nonviolence are more than ever relevant for today's crisis-ridden and morally fractured world. As we are face-to-face with a crisis in civilization ,Lord Buddha and his teachings seem to be the last refuge and panacea for humanity.

REFERENCES

- Ambedkar, B.R. 1996. *Bauddha Dharma O Darshan*. Mahabodhi Book Agency, Kolkata.

- Barua, Dipak Kumar. 2015. *Buddhist Philosophy*. Createspace Publishing, California, USA.

- Brammachary, Pandit Silananda. 2011. *Mahasanti Mahaprem*. Kolkata: Maha Bodhi Book Agency.

- Das, Asha. 2013. *Bauddha Darshan O Rabindranath*. India: Mahabodhi Book Agency, Kolkata- 73.

- Das, Asha, 2014. *Indian Philosophy & Buddhism*. Mahabodhi Book Agency, Kolkata-73.

- Mahasthavir, Pandit Dharmadar. 1994. *Dhammapada*, Dharmadhar Bouddha Grantha Prakasani, Calcutta-15.

- Sankrityayan, Mahapandita Rahul. 1989, Buddhist Philosophy. Moscow: Lenin University.

- Sen, Ranabrata, ed. 1968. *Dhammapada*, Haraf Prakasani, Kolkata.

- Tagore, Rabindranathi. 1984. *Maitri Bhavana o Bauddha Darshan*. Shantiniketan, India: Visva Bharati University.

- Vivekananda, Swami. 1996. *Buddha o Bauddha Dharma*, 8th ed. West Bengal, India: Belur Math.

- Quayum, Mohammad A. May 2, 2017. *War, Violence and Rabindranath Tagore's Quest for World Peace,* Malaysia: Transnational Literature, vol. 9, https://researchnow- admin.flinders.edu.au/ws/files/29249665/Quayum_War_P2017.pdf

BUDDHISM AND WORLD PEACE

Dr. Swarnali Barua

Assistant Professor, Presidency University, Kolkata, India

*A*s we have entered the twenty-first century, the world has been witnessing an increasing number of conflicts and wars globally. While such global disputes occur due to corruption, financial scams, unequal distribution of wealth, one of the principal reasons behind conflicts in different parts of the world today have been due to religious extremism. Several underdeveloped and developing counties like Afghanistan, Iraq, parts of Africa, Bangladesh, India, and many other parts of the world have been suffering due to extreme terrorisms. Even in the developed countries like USA, Germany, UK, several cases of shootouts are being reported almost every day. Russia and Ukraine are currently at war with each other. The impact of such wars is severe. It brings distress and death without any distinction.

According to the United Nations, there are presently 70 million people living away from their home because of war. Wars have a negative influence on the physical health of the civilians, as well as a negative impact on the mental health of both combatants and civilians. War and violence create a vicious dysfunctional cycle, a deadly trap that primarily impacts civilians, especially the children. Children do not lead typical lives in places where there are wars or other armed crises. They see the destruction of their homes and the harm or death of their loved ones, neighbors, and friends. Such incidents may leave severe trauma on the mental health of the children and affect their emotional behavior towards other people.

Even if the wars and conflicts are widespread, its inception can be linked to individual choices. Wars start when one nation's citizens, or its rulers, have unsatisfied desires, are arrogant or have greed for wealth or power, or they are enraged or hostile. Racial or national arrogance is another way that this might appear. They mistakenly believe that using force to solve problems that are largely internal to their own minds can solve them. Such irrational decisions ultimately are taken when one's mind is not at peace with or one is not satisfied with one's own self. This is where following the philosophy of Buddha can help an individual to bring the peace within. Until and unless humans find peace within themselves, they will not be at peace with their surroundings and commit violence, conflicts, and harm the people around. Such actions create disturbance in society, creating suffering among the people.

Peace is not just the absence of any conflict or animosity; it is rather the presence of serenity and happiness. In order for people to live happy and satisfied lives, the citizens of a nation need to have their own social and economic well-being. It is also important that all the nations try to maintain good relationships among each other and live in harmony for any kind of social, economic, or political well-being and development. The teachings of Buddha will help in achieving such harmonious coexistence, not only among the people of a nation, but also among the different nations.

Practicing the principles of the Buddha teaches one to have self-control, self-restraint, and tolerance. The teaching of the Buddha is based on having compassion for other living beings irrespective of any kind of social barriers and differences. It teaches us humanism. This is why Buddhism was accepted by some people in ancient India when there was a rise in social tensions, oppression of the poor by the powerful class and discrimination among people based on their caste, gender, and color. Buddha "could offer to the people of his times the illusion of liberty, equality and fraternity, which, as the inevitable result of the laws of social advance, were being trampled and undermined in reality (Saksena, www.ayk.govt.tr). The Buddha was only responding to such circumstances as an unknowing tool of history, and Buddhism was destined from its birth to become one of the largest socio-religious movements in Indian history.

Many rulers and emperors in India such as Bimbisara, Ashoka, and Kanishka embraced Buddhism and propagated its teaching to other South Asian countries. Even in modern India several great men and scholars like Swami Vivekananda, Dr. Babasaheb Ambedkar, and Mahatma Gandhi believed in the philosophy of Buddhism. Mahatma Gandhi followed and used the principals of nonviolence or *ahimsa*, which led to the freedom of India from the British rulers. Even the makers of the Indian constitution understood the importance of Buddhism in promoting peace, harmony, and tolerance in a country like India, where people with different ideologies, religions, castes, creeds, colors and cultures have been co-existing for ages. Hence, the principal of *panchashila* was considered in the making of different policies of the constitution. The five precepts are abstaining from killing other living beings, from stealing, from misconduct, from lying and intoxication. If these precepts are practiced by the individuals of the society, then in such a society there will not be any kind of crimes, hatred, and violence.

Nonviolence in both thoughts and actions is one of the main

principals of Buddhism. The first precept of *panchashila* states that killing and harming other living organisms should be avoided. The followers of the Buddha believe that cultivating loving-kindness and compassion instead of repressing emotions like anger is the only way for people to live in peace and harmony.

According to the Dhammapada: Pairs, Verse 5: "Hatred is never appeased by hatred in this world. By non-hatred alone is hatred appeased. This is a law eternal." (Fronsdal, 2006). The Buddha taught that ignorance is the root cause of all suffering. The fundamental ignorance is our inability to recognize that the self, which occupies the center of all of our existence, shapes how we perceive the outside world, and guides our activities for our convenience and benefit, is an illusion. All of our misery is a result of this self-illusion and selfishness. We are poisoned by desires and greed when we are selfish. We frequently experience anger and hatred when they are not fulfilled. These fundamental emotional states block us from accessing our own innate wisdom and compassion as well as the radiant depths of our minds. Such minds bring disturbance and conflicts in our society.

Buddhism teaches a human must simultaneously cultivate the virtues of wisdom and compassion. In this context, wisdom implies the intellectual side of the mind, while compassion would represent traits like love, kindness, and tolerance on the emotional side. A good-hearted person may result from developing only the emotional part of oneself while neglecting the intellectual; on the other hand, a hard-hearted intelligence without empathy may result from developing only the intellectual side. So, in order to be perfect, one must equally develop both. Following the Noble Eightfold Path given by the Buddha will help us to develop such virtues.

The Noble Eightfold Path, which forms the foundation of Buddhism, is believed to have been created with the goal of bringing happiness and serenity to both individuals and society. Right vision enables one to satisfy desire, which is the source of all suffering, and directs one towards the way of serenity. Right thought suggests one should see things as they are, not as one expects. Right aim prevents one from desiring wealth and power at the expense of others or indulging in senses and luxury. It also enables one to have the capability to love people and make them happier. Right speech implies cautions against using one's tongue carelessly which may result in violence and murder. Proper speech is truthful, friendly, and controlled. Right action and livelihood suggest avoiding hazardous behaviors like murder, theft, adultery, and other wrongdoing with the goal of doing good things that would benefit other people. Right mindfulness and the right concentration give the path towards liberation from suffering. It is achieved through meditation. Following steps in the Eightfold Path urges us to purge evils from our minds and cultivate good thoughts in order to bring harmony and happiness to society.

For a happy and calm mind, one must develop a compassionate attitude. True compassion is based on the needs of others rather than our own expectations. Whether the other person is a friend or a rival, as long as we desire peace, happiness, and the end of suffering, we can develop genuine concern for the problem they are experiencing. To develop such compassion is not easy to achieve, it needs mind training. We can cultivate the positive aspects of our thoughts, attitudes, and perspectives while minimizing the negative thoughts. We must make a conscious effort to make our mind rational and convince our mind to make positive changes and develop empathy for other living beings. Our personal sorrow is made more bearable by keeping in mind the suffering of others and by having empathy for them.

According to the Dalai Lama, the development of compassion is the key to a better and more prosperous world at every level of society, be it in a family or national or international level. He says that we do not require to adopt a specific ideology or to adopt a particular religion for development of a compassionate attitude. All that is required from every one of us is that we grow in our positive human traits. Cultivating personal happiness can make a significant and powerful contribution to the general uplift of the entire human community. Since we are all human, this earth is our sole home, each of us needs to have a strong feeling of universal kindness and compassion if we're going to safeguard our home from wars and conflicts.

Buddhism is a time-tested scientific religion built on spiritual as well as logical reasoning. It is based more on practice rather than faith. Practicing the philosophy of Buddhism in our life has become absolute necessary in the present times to maintain global peace. The Buddha's teachings offer practical methods for controlling rage, restraining desires, and establishing peaceful relationships. Currently in a world full of violence and corruption, people need peace and understanding from a spiritual path that teaches nonviolence, serenity, compassion, generosity of spirit, and peace of mind. Buddhism encourages us to develop inner peace and try to reduce suffering in all living things, which ultimately is necessary to maintain peace in the world.

REFERENCES

- Encyclopædia of Religion and Ethics. (2022, November 7). In Wikipedia. https://en.wikipedia.org/wiki/Encyclop%C3%A6dia_of_Religion_and_Ethics

- Fronsdal, Gil. 2006. The Dhammapada: A New Translation of the Buddhist Classic with Annotations. Colorado: Shambhala Publications.

- Raghuvira and Lokesh Chandra, 2 vols A Comprehensive English-Hindi dictionary, supplementary volume (Satapitaka Series: 625). Published by Aditya Prakashan, New Delhi, 2009.

- Saksana, Rakesh. 2002. Buddhism and Its Message of Peace. https://www.ayk.gov.tr/wp- content/uploads/2015/01/SAKSANA-Rakesh-Buddhism-and-Its-Message-of-Peace.pdf

- Tenzin Gyatso; the Fourteenth Dalai Lama. "Compassion

and the Individual." Accessed August 9, 2023. www.dalailama.com/messages/compassion-and-human-values/compassion.

DHAMMA:
THE GREAT GIFT TO MANKIND

Subhajit Chatterjee, PhD

Independent Researcher, Japanese Studies

Shantiniketan, India

*B*uddhism today represents the largest field of thought in the known history of mankind. Its components are partly visible and partly invisible, the former including a long and complex story of 2,500 years of development combined with what may be called the geography of Buddhism, in the course of time at least a dozen countries. Races and cultures came under its sway and its story and scriptures are written in at least seven different languages.

Buddhism is the most important religion historically, not

philosophically-because it was the most tremendous religious movement that the world had ever seen. It was the most gigantic spiritual wave ever to burst upon human society; there is no civilization on which its effect has not been felt in some way or other. Meanwhile, what seems to be the oldest school of Buddhism, the Theravada, which alone survived of the eighteen subdivisions of the Hinayana, was firmly established and flourished today in Sri Lanka, Burma, and Thailand. Yet in terms of numbers and geographical area, the Theravada covers less than half the Buddhist field, for the Dhamma was carried east to China, Korea, and Japan; north into Tibet and Mongolia and the expanded teaching known as the Mahayana was at one time a powerful factor in a thousand million minds.

In Sikkim the movement is well re-established while it is growing, though slowly, in Nepal largely thanks to the effort of the Ven. Amritananda, who organized the Congress of the World Fellowship of Buddhists in Katmandu in November 1956. Ladakh and Bhutan are still virtually closed to foreigners and the growth of Buddhism therein is problematical. In Tibet there is such powerful resistance to Chinese efforts to purge the nation of its spiritual heritage. More than that one cannot say, but all who have had the privilege of meeting the Dalai Lama, now living in India, will agree that the present holder of that office is a man of great spiritual power and adored by his people.

In China the flame of Buddhism burns low but is far from being extinguished. A group of Chinese Buddhists from Peking who attended a recent Congress of the World Fellowship of Buddhists were unanimous in stating that they had complete freedom for research propaganda, and Buddhist Institutions of one kind or another are being opened in various parts of the enormous country. In South Korea Buddhism is still soundly established.

Japan is rising rapidly in every field, and in friendly and useful contacts with the western world. Here Buddhism is strong, mostly of the Shin and Zen sects, but with an amazing number of Buddhist groups of every kind springing up spontaneously in various parts of the country.

The government of India, as a first step after independence, adopted Dhamma Chakka, popularly known as the Ashok Chakra as the national emblem in the year 1955 in Banding Indonesia when a conference of twenty-nine states of Asia and Africa was called for peace and unity. It was at the insistence of the late Pandit Jawahar Lal Nehru.

Simultaneously, there were more than five million Hindy outcasts who voluntarily embraced the religion in 1956 in Nagpur under the leadership of late Dr. Ambedkar. Buddhism came west, back to India whence it had been expelled in the tenth to twelfth centuries. In the work of the Maha Bodhi Society, which has centers in all the great cities, and in the work of the late Dr. Ambedkar, among the "untouchables there are signs of a movement which may yet profoundly affect the face of India."

Buddhism continued west to Europe and the USA.

Finally, those very few with sufficient breadth of mind to appreciate the range and splendor of the Buddhist field must actively help the headquarters of the Fellowship wherever situated, to organize succeeding conferences for the fearless study of Buddhism in all its variety, for objective comparison between its forms and for methods of offering Buddhist teaching to the modern world of science and social service in the form most suitable.

But where are these few, and how can they be encouraged to appear?

I believe that enough exist to make that attempt at formulating a World Buddhism worth their while and if strongly encouraged their number may grow. After all, is there any greater gift to mankind than the Dhamma, and if we offer it, why not all of it? And to all?

REFERENCES

Books

- Appleton, Naomi. 2010. *Jātaka Stories in Theravāda Buddhism: Narrating the Bodhisatta Path*. U n i t e d Kingdom: Ashgate Publishing Limited.

- Babbitt, Ellen C. 1912. *The Jatakas: Tales of India: Retold by Ellen C. Babbitt*. New York: The Century Company.

- Chopra, Deepak. 2007. *Buddha: A Story of Enlightenment*. London: Harper Collins.

- Davids, T.W. Rhys and Oldenberg Hermann. 1968. *Vinaya Texts Translated from the Pāli,   Part I: The Paimokkha, The Mahavaga, I-IV; Part II: The Mahavagga (V–X), The   Kullavagga I–III)*. New York: Charles Scribner's Sons, 1899; Republished in 1968 by Motilal Banarsidass (*Sacred Books of the East Series*), Delhi, India.

- Finnigan, Bronwyn. 2017. "Buddhism and Animal Ethics." ResearchGate,   w w w . r e s e a r c h g a t e . n e t . Accessed May 5, 2023.   https://www.researchgate. net/publication/316738919_Buddhism_and_Animal

- Francis, H. T. and E. J. Thomas. 1916. *Jātaka Tales: Selected and Edited with Introduction and   Notes*. Cambridge: University Press.

- Gyatso, Bhikṣu Tenzin (The Fourteenth Dalai Lama) and Bhikṣuṇī Thubten Chodron. 2014. *Buddhism: One Teacher, Many Traditions*. Boston: Wisdom Publications.

- Hazra, Kanai Lal. 1982. *History of Theravāda Buddhism in South-East Asia*. New Delhi, India: Munshiram Manoharlal Publishers.

- Wilson, Jeff. 2009. *Buddhism of the Heart: Reflections on Shin Buddhism and Inner   T o g e t h e r n e s s*. Massachusetts: Wisdom Publications

Ethics

- Santucci, James A. 2002. "A Theravāda Buddhist Contribution to Universal Ethics." *The Hsi Lai Journal of Humanistic Buddhism.* Accessed May 5, 2023, buddhism.lib.ntu.edu.tw; http://buddhism.lib.ntu.edu.tw/ FULLTEXT/JR-   MAG/mag353948.pdf

- Tomalin, Emma. 2007. "Buddhism and Development: A Background Paper." ResearchGate. Accessed April 6, 2023.   https://www.researchgate. net/publication/239591881_Buddhism_and_   pment_A_ Background_Paper

Articles

- Srivichai, Suddipong. 2017. "Buddhist Perspectives and World Peace." *International Journal of Multidisciplinary Management and Tourism.* Vol. 1 No. 1 January – June 2017.

THE ROLE OF BUDDHISM IN INDIA'S SOFT POWER DIPLOMACY AND WORLD PEACE

Saurav Barua

A Devotee, Durganagar, Kolkata, India

*B*uddhism is one of the religions in which there doesn't have to be any kind of radicalization or misogynistic problems; there is no discrimination and no violence at all. It's a religion that has human rights, women's rights, freedom of speech, and gender equality which a peaceful world really needs. We can say it's a kind of secular religion in which every human has the same freedom of rights.

Every other religion can follow Buddhism easily; there are no obstructions or any kind of religious dogma one has to believe or rules to follow. We can easily make Buddhist practices a part of our lives and the Buddha offered many suggestions for doing this. He taught us how to stop suffering and gave us precise instructions for accomplishing this. These instructions-this Buddhist way of life-leads to a happy life. Buddhist teachings taught us how to treat everyone equally, how to be kind to others, and how to be compassionate to every living being. The teaching and path the Buddha taught can be followed by every human being. Following the path will result in being successful, as well as being a good human being.

The term "soft power" was coined by Joseph Nye in the 1990s. He defined soft power as the ability to get what you want through attraction rather than coercion or payments. Its major characteristics are value, cultures, and policies. So, what major role does a religion like Buddhism play in India's soft power diplomacy? At the very first, we have to understand the reality behind Buddhism and the historical connection between India and the religion of Buddhism.

Siddhartha Gautama, the founder of Buddhism, was born in Lumbini in 560 BCE. He was a great philosopher, a prince of the Sakhya Dynasty of Kapilabastu and son of King Suddhodhana and Queen Mayadevi. Right from his birth, the young prince was surrounded by wealth and great privileges. He was destined to become king of one of the most important royal families in the region. Yet as he grew older and more mature, he began to question many aspects of the princely life. Finally, he became so totally disillusioned with the ostentatious wealth and power of the Sakhyas that he felt compelled to abandon his royal heritage and become an ascetic.

One day the prince left his palace to know the reality which was hidden from him. Born as a prince, Siddhartha was confined within the palace walls until he grew up. He never saw the outer world. One day he ventured out and saw the death, illnesses, and sufferings of people. Stirred by what he saw, he decided to return to the palace. On his way back, through the woods, he chanced upon a monk who was blissfully meditating under a tree. Siddhartha noticed that the monk had no possessions with him. He only wrapped himself in a simple cloth. Siddhartha contemplated that he was a prince who had everything, every luxury and comfort but still felt a void inside. But here was this monk with nothing but tranquility on his face.

Siddhartha wisely concluded that the monk must have attained something that made him fulfilled even while having no worldly possessions. The suffering he witnessed prior also made him question the permanency and goal of human life. Hence, to solve these questions and find the truth he left his palace and everything else in it. So from here what we have learned? The world is very big and beyond our imagination; we cannot realize the reality without seeing the outer world, without facing the real problems that other individuals are facing. We should not have to be confined within our comfort zone. Our worldly possessions are temporary; we cannot take them with us when we die, but our every reaction to every action spiritually will make us immortal to the world. Do everything with a good heart and expect nothing in return.

What is Buddhism? Is it only a religion pioneered by Siddhartha Gautama? Or something else? Buddhism is simply a way of life. In Buddhism it is believed that human life is one of suffering and that meditation, spiritual and physical labor, and good behavior are the ways to achieve enlightenment or Nirvana. Buddhism teaches us that all beings in the universe are subject to certain natural laws and, moreover, that they are trapped in an endless round of existences. Death is just one phase of this cycle and is repeatedly followed by rebirth which is yet another phase of this endless round.

All of us who are caught up in the Wheel of Life will continue the cycle almost indefinitely until such time as we are able to realize the unsatisfactory nature of our existences and to relinquish our desires. At this moment, there will no longer be the desire to continue and, by letting go, we break the cycle of continuity forever. This is the ultimate state to which all Buddhists aspire-the attainment of enlightenment. The path to the realization of enlightenment is the avoidance of extremes in life. The "Middle Way" is the Buddhist way of life; a self-development progression through the Noble Eightfold Path which comprises Right Understanding, Right Thought, Right Speech, Right Action, Right Livelihood, Right

Effort, Right Mindfulness, and Right Concentration.

Siddhartha Gautama finally reached enlightenment under the shadow of a tree at Bodh Gaya in Bihar and from there the spiritual journey of Gautama Buddha began. He reached Saranath and preached his first sermon known as the "Dhamma Chakra Pravartana." He then traveled primarily around northern India, mainly in the regions of UP and Bihar, met various kings and preached to them the truth of life, taking them into the fold.

Buddha preached his knowledge until 460 BCE when in Kushinagar, he left his mortal body and reached Tushita (Buddhist heaven). After the *mahaparinirvana* of Buddha, the first Buddhist council was held by Ajatshatru, the king of Magadha in Rajgir. The most influential kings were the Great Asoka of Mauryas and the Kanishka of Kushans. It was Asoka who started to propagate Buddhism in countries outside of India. He sent his daughter Sanghamitra and son Mahendra to Sri Lanka. He appointed Dharma *rajjikas* to look into this matter officially.

In later times, the first century CE, Kanishka the Kushan ruler captured the silk route of China and started propagating Buddhism in regions of China. From this point of initiation, we can see in further times Kumargupta will be building Nalanda University which will become a famous Buddhist monastery. Pala rulers will be building other monasteries, such as Vikramshila, Odnatpuri, and Jagdalla. These monasteries became the source of Tibetan Buddhism finally reaching to the core of China, Japan, and Korea regions. There was not only outflow-Chinese missionaries came to India to visit the Buddhist side. During Chandragupta II, Fa Hien came; during Harsha's reign, Huen Tsang came; and in later times It Sing, Wang Xuan, and other travelers came to India. They learned extensively about Buddhism and propagated it in their motherland.

India has a spiritual legacy when it comes to Buddhism and Indian policy makers want to use this in order to project India's soft power. Buddhism's influence is actually evident in Indian architecture, painting, culture and even the Ashokan pillar (the national emblem of India) of Sarnath from the Mauryan Era.

The dharma wheel in India's flag is also a Buddhist heritage. The Buddhist faith originated in India, therefore granting it singular historical legitimacy.

India has numerous sites of importance to the Buddhist faith, such as Bodh Gaya, Sarnath, and Nalanda. India has nurtured an image of being a protector of the persecuted because of the presence of the Dalai Lama and the Tibetan parliament-in-exile in the city of Dharamshala following their failed insurrection against China. In addition to ties with Tibetan Buddhism, historical links to Theravada Buddhism mean that India is in a good position to further relations with other Buddhist countries and create a conversation between multiple streams of this faith.

The Panchasheel Agreement that India signed with China was based on five Buddhist principles and was supposed to breed friendly and positive relations between India and China. Chinese occupation of Tibet is also something that India wouldn't be looking ahead into and hence India built her own narrative surrounding Buddhism. India does have credible stakes to Buddhism. That Buddhism originated in India gives singular historical legitimacy to Indian claims. One of India's most important initiatives is the Buddhist Circuit to promote soft power. An example of this is India developing better tourist infrastructure at all the Buddhist pilgrimage sites.

Buddhist Circuit Initiative of India

- Lumbini, Nepal – Siddhartha Gautama's (Buddha's) birthplace

- Kapilavastu, Uttar Pradesh – The place where Gautama Buddha spent his early years as Siddhartha.

- Bodh Gaya, Bihar – The place where Gautama Buddha attained enlightenment.

- Sarnath, Varanasi, Uttar Pradesh – Site of the Buddha's first sermon, his first teaching after attaining enlightenment.

- Rajgir, Bihar – This is where Buddha lived and taught. He preached his two most famous sermons here.

- Kausambi, Uttar Pradesh – Kausambi is the place where Lord Buddha stayed and preached in the sixth and ninth years after having attained enlightenment.

- Shravasti, Uttar Pradesh – Buddha spent twenty-four rainy seasons here.

- Vaishali, Bihar – The place where Gautama Buddha attained *parinirvana* is commonly used to refer to Nirvana-after-death, which occurs upon the death of someone who has attained Nirvana during his or her lifetime.

- Kushinagar, Uttar Pradesh – The place where Gautama Buddha attained parinirvana. Parinirvana is commonly used to refer to Nirvana-after-death which occurs upon the death of someone who has attained Nirvana in his or her lifetime.

Why does Buddhism play a major role in the soft power diplomacy of India?

The answer lies in the mutual consideration amongst most Asian countries. The shared cultural values of Buddhism find resonance within most of the major parts of the continent. Asian countries as of today consist of around 97 percent of the Buddhist population in the world, with over fourteen countries having more than 50 percent of their populations preaching Buddhism, while seven of those nations have 90 percent of their citizens practicing Buddhism as their primary religion. The countries influenced by Buddhism range from Nepal, Tibet, Mongolia, Myanmar, Sri Lanka, and Central Asia to even countries in the Nordic regions as well. However, countries like Cambodia, Thailand, Malaysia, Laos, Japan, Vietnam, Singapore, South Korea, and others in the region constitute a major Buddhist- populated block. Buddhism contributes to enriching the soft power of India. The development of Buddhism creates a cultural link between India and the world, helping to expand the influence of India by the power of culture and religious faith. Through Buddhism, people know and admire India as an ancient culture of the East.

The use of soft power in the form of Buddhism is not new to

a country like India. As we saw in the introduction of Buddhism, Asoka used Buddhism as a soft power in Sri Lanka and Kanishka in China regions. Later on, Chola kings in the tenth century also allowed the formation of monasteries in India for Buddhist monks led this cultural expansion. The Pala Dynasty was one of the dynasties in early medieval India that led to Buddhism integrating into Tibet regions completely and migrating to other regions. This revival of Buddhism's potential utility in modern foreign policy was facilitated by the foundation of several organizations and the convening of numerous councils and conferences in the decades after the Second World War. These emphasized transnational cooperation amongst various sects of Buddhism. This began with a conference organized in newly independent Sri Lanka, where the World Fellowship of Buddhists was founded. In 1952, under the prime ministership of Jawaharlal Nehru, India hosted the International Buddhist Conference in Sanchi which was attended by over 3,000 Buddhist nuns, monks, and historians. In 1954, the Sixth Buddhist Council was convened in Burma which Baba Saheb Ambedkar presided over.

In 2016, the fifteenth International Buddhist Conclave was organized in Varanasi by the Indian Tourism Ministry with attendees from thirty-nine countries all over the world. These things gave India a special legitimacy. In fact, the government of India especially emphasizes the shared Buddhist heritage and certain initiatives had been taken in the academic world as well. For example, the launch of Nalanda University was an initiative funded by multiple Asian countries. Buddhism is an intrinsic part of India's spiritual heritage.

Importance of Youth Involvement in Buddhism

Now we will discuss the reason behind the importance of youth involvement in Buddhism. We all are aware that youths are future leaders. The youth of today are the leaders of tomorrow. The involvement of youth is important to strengthen the root of religion as well. This young generation is the largest consumer of information and they are very much updated with our current world and can easily coordinate with every level of people. Youth is a stage on which they serve as connectors between children and adults. Aside from providing an environment for young people, the role of youth in a religion can also involve helping the elderly in the community. They can also participate in other services in religious institutions and help older members in their spiritual search. The youth are the future of a religion and are often the ones who will determine whether to follow the traditions of the past or introduce something new. The youth are also the best resource for ensuring that religious institutions don't become extinct. They can provide fresh perspectives on the things they see and experience. They can be the pillars of any institution and key to its growth and development. The youth can also lead small groups. This is a great way to create a strong bond. The youth will also be a valuable part of the congregation.

As we discussed, the benefit of involvement of youths in religious institutions is good for a religion. It is also important for the youth to connect with spirituality and to practice it in a serial way, and a religious institution is the best place to do that. Currently, youths are facing various kinds of problems in their lives. They are the victims of depression and anxiety, so they become unmindful, forgetful, and negligent in their nature. In addition to the Buddha's advice on preventing and handling depression, meditation is the only way to get rid of this-meditation meaning the act of giving one's attention to only one thing as a way of becoming calm and relaxed. In particular, mindfulness meditation and loving-kindness meditation are found to be of great help in preventing and treating depression.

REFERENCES

- Indian history and Indian art culture notes for civil services given by Sahojpath Institute.

WORLD PEACE THROUGH BUDDHISM

Subhankar Barua

Employment Officer, WBCS Group-A WBES

Labor Department, Government of West Bengal

Member of Young Buddhist Association, Jetaban Buddha Bihar

*B*uddhism is generally regarded, with good reason, as the most peaceful of world religions. It stresses the principle of *ahimsa,* the "non-injury" of other living things. Buddhism is an outstanding religious theological tradition for promoting world peace and harmony based on the philosophy of philanthropic humanism and universal fraternity, which is a hallmark of Lord Buddha's teachings transcending all national racial, social, and cultural barriers. This twenty-first century where the clock is ticking with modern lifelines, where we are actually living in a state of contradictions, ambiguities, and inbuilt anxieties that are said to be a landmark of modern times. In the present context of the world, which is shattered by poverty, unemployment, social crisis, long-lasting greed and war, it seems that war has become propaganda to cultivate the economy in drastic ways. *Hingsha* transformed into a modern mode of attacking peace, to destroy other's happiness.

The ages of society saw the most momentous social upheavals in the world. Sociopolitical life, the transition from small social groups to state, formation of the army, emerging merchant classes with concomitant social vices characteristic of commercialism. This leads to the ever- building contrary and anything contrary to this would result in disturbing one's peace and lead to conflict. The war between Ukraine-Russia, political conflict between US-Iran, terrorist activities, and all this is only for the contradiction that who will play a major role in geopolitics. Amidst the tension generated by these, humans fall from liberty, equality, and fraternity. The hope and need for world peace is replaced by silence.

"Peace" or "shanti" is not just the absence of war or hostility, but rather it is *santisukha*, which is accompanied by tranquility and happiness. Peace in a state does not only mean that there is no conflict. It also means allowing citizens to develop their own social and economic well-being in order to live a happy life. So peace and happiness must go hand in hand. There cannot be true peace without real happiness. It also proposes that peace in society is a very tangible goal. Achieving peace is obtainable and it is a responsibility. Nowadays, most agree that peace is no more a stable state to be reached at the end of the tunnel, but a composite of dynamic interactions demanding continued striving because of the constantly changing conditions of all forces and factors involved.

It was Buddha who provided a substitute. People want to live an ultimately happy life with no harm toward themselves. The Buddha teaches they should start with avoiding causing harm to others, physically and verbally at the personal level.

Buddhism as a social code leads us to peace, understanding, and integration. Buddha tried to inculcate in his followers the sense of service and understanding with love and compassion by separating humans from passion and elevating humanistic tendencies with the help of morality, *karuna* and *samata*. In formulating the theoretical basis of his dhamma, Buddha looked upon the suffering of his age as a sickness, a disease. The *arya satyas* which he pronounced were concerned with suffering. Buddha raised the concrete material sufferings. The ultimate problem of all human suffering was traced to ignorance and the problem was solved simply by removing it from the realm of reality through the principle of dhamma. This tells us about the core of Buddhism i.e., the Noble Eightfold Path was formulated to bring happiness and peace not only to the individuals, but to society at large.

The view of peace as a collective product is well in line with the Buddhist worldview based on the principle of dependent origination which emphasizes the mutual influence of all the elements involved in any situation. Yet its teachings also emphasize that violence harms the spiritual state of the perpetrator, as well as the victim. Malicious thoughts or deeds are regarded as obstacles on the path to Nirvana, the self-transcendence which is the endpoint of all spiritual endeavors. With this interdependent frame of reference, Buddhists would prefer a holistic view of peace, instead of just focusing on individual peace.

At the international level, nations are supposed to develop their own social, economic, political, and self-reliance for the well-being of their people. At the same time, they have to be conscious of what is going on beyond their own borders and contribute to the maintenance of world peace. Without world peace, it is impossible to achieve the tranquility and harmony needed for nations' development and progress. In the changing world of today, Buddhism has a great deal to contribute to establishing peace. It provides for a revolutionary doctrine of peace by way of a concept of commonwealth of dharma.

Sabbe satta sukhita hontu
Sabbe dukhya gamochantu
May all beings be happy.

REFERENCES

- Barua, Dipak Kumar. 2015. *Buddhist Philosophy.* Createspace Publishing, California, USA.

- *Brainwave: A Multidisciplinary Journal*, Volumes 1, 2, , 4, 5.

- Mahasthavir, Pandit Dharmadar. 1994. *Dhammapada*, Dharmadhar Bouddha Grantha Prakasani, Calcutta.

- Sen, Ranabrata, ed. 1968. *Dhammapada*, Haraf Prakasani, Kolkata.

- Sherab, Khenchen Palden Rinpoche and Dongyal, Khenpo Tsewang Dongyal Rinpoche. 1997. *The Light of Peace,* 2nd ed. New York: Padmasambhava Buddhist Centre, 7, 13, 22.

- Sherab, Khenchen Palden Rinpoche and Dongyal, Khenpo Tsewang Dongyal Rinpoche. 2019. *The Light of Peace: How Buddhism Shines in the World,* New York: Padmasambhava   Buddhist Centre.

- Tagore, Rabindranathi. 1984. *Maitri Bhavana O Bauddha Darshan.* Shantiniketan, India: Visva   B h a r a t i University.

- Vivekananda, Swami. 1996. *Buddha o Bauddha Dharma*, 8th ed. West Bengal, India: Belur Math.

BUDDHIST IDEAS FOR WORLD PEACE:CULTIVATING HARMONY AND COMPASSION

Pradyut Chowdhuri

General Secretary, Rishra Bauddha Samity

Rishra, W.B. India

Introduction

𝒥n a world rife with conflicts and strife, the pursuit of global peace remains an enduring aspiration. Buddhism, a philosophy and spiritual tradition with roots in ancient India, offers profound insights and practices that can contribute to the attainment of global harmony. With its emphasis on compassion, mindfulness, and the interconnectedness of all beings, Buddhism provides a unique perspective on achieving peace at both the individual and collective levels. This article explores the fundamental teachings of Buddhism, its core principles, and how they can be applied to foster peace and understanding in the world.

The Core Tenets of Buddhism

At the heart of Buddhism lies the Four Noble Truths, which acknowledge the existence of suffering, its origin, the possibility of liberation from suffering, and the path to achieving it. The path to liberation, known as the Noble Eightfold Path, includes right understanding, intention, speech, action, livelihood, effort, mindfulness, and concentration. Through acts of kindness, forgiveness, and empathy, individuals can cultivate a compassionate mindset and extend it to others, fostering peace in their immediate surroundings and beyond.

Compassion as the Foundation

Buddhists recognize that all beings are interconnected and that our actions have repercussions that extend beyond ourselves. This awareness fosters a sense of responsibility and compassion towards others. Buddhism teaches that true happiness and peace can be found through the alleviation of suffering in others, as well as in ourselves. By cultivating compassion and engaging in acts of kindness, Buddhists work towards the well-being of all sentient beings. Through acts of kindness, forgiveness, and empathy, individuals can cultivate a compassionate mindset and extend it to others, fostering peace in their immediate surroundings and beyond.

Mindfulness and Inner Peace

Mindfulness, another vital aspect of Buddhism, involves being fully present and aware of one's thoughts, feelings, and surroundings. By practicing mindfulness, individuals can develop a deep understanding of their own minds and emotions. This self-awareness allows them to respond to challenging situations with equanimity, promoting peace within themselves and in their interactions with others. When people find peace within themselves, they become more equipped to respond to conflicts and challenges with clarity and compassion, thus contributing to the promotion of peace in the world.

Nonviolence and Conflict Resolution

Engaged Buddhism is a concept that encourages Buddhists to actively participate in the betterment of society and work for social justice. Engaged Buddhists strive to alleviate suffering and promote peace by addressing social, economic, and environmental issues. They advocate for equality, compassion, and ethical conduct in all aspects of life. Engaged Buddhist practitioners often engage in humanitarian work, promote education, support nonprofit organizations, and participate in peace-building initiatives. By actively working to address the causes of suffering and promoting justice, Engaged Buddhists contribute to the realization of world peace.

Buddhist Practices for World Peace

Buddhism offers several practices that can contribute to the realization of global peace. Meditation, a cornerstone of Buddhist practice, helps individuals develop inner calm and clarity. By cultivating a peaceful state of mind through meditation, individuals become more capable of responding to conflicts with wisdom and compassion.

Engaging in *metta* meditation, or the practice of loving-kindness is another way Buddhists promote peace. This practice involves generating feelings of love, compassion, and goodwill towards oneself, loved ones, neutral individuals, and even adversaries. By cultivating these qualities, practitioners seek to dissolve hostility and generate an atmosphere of understanding and reconciliation.

Buddha realized that peace would come only when humans are happy. Buddha wanted humans to get rid of all malice, hatred, indulgence in lower desires, and evil thoughts. Buddha wanted to substitute these with good thoughts, worthy desires, feelings of charity and compassion, and an attitude of serenity and composure.

Furthermore, Buddhist principles encourage ethical behavior and social responsibility. The Five Precepts, which include refraining from harming living beings, stealing, engaging in sexual misconduct, false speech, and intoxication serve as guidelines for leading an ethical life. By adhering to these precepts, individuals contribute to a more peaceful and just society.

Engaged Buddhism

Engaged Buddhism is a concept that encourages Buddhists to actively participate in the betterment of society and work for social justice. They advocate for equality, compassion, and ethical conduct in all aspects of life. Engaged Buddhist practitioners often engage in humanitarian work, promote education, support nonprofit organizations, and participate in peace-building initiatives. By actively working to address the causes of suffering and promoting justice, Engaged Buddhists contribute to the realization of world peace.

Conclusion

Buddhist ideas offer a comprehensive and holistic approach to attaining world peace. By cultivating compassion, practicing mindfulness, embracing nonviolence, recognizing interconnectedness, developing wisdom, and engaging in compassionate action, individuals and societies can work towards a more peaceful and harmonious world. The teachings of Buddhism remind us of the inherent potential for peace within each individual and encourage us to extend that peace to others. As we collectively embrace these ideas, we move closer to the realization of a world where compassion, understanding, and harmony prevail.

REFERENCES

- Barua, Rudiak Kumar, 1998, *Buddhist Philosophy*. India.
- Das, Asha. 2013. *Bauddha Darshan O Rabindranath*. India: Mahabodhi Book Agency, Kolkata- 73.
- *Brainwave: A Multidisciplinary Journal*, Volumes 1–5.
- Mahasthavir, Pandit Dharmadar. 1994. *Dhammapada*,

BUDDHISM FOR WORLD PEACE AND HARMONY

Madhumita Barua

A Devotee, Satragachhi, West Bengal

To begin with, I extend my heartfelt thanks to the organizers for giving me an opportunity to speak on today's topic, "Contributions of Buddhism for World Peace and Harmony."

First of all, I feel extremely lucky that I have been born in India, the holy land where Lord Budda attained Nirvana. Buddhism is the gospel of peace, nonviolence and harmony which emanates from the eradication of the six vices of mankind. Nonviolence teaches mankind to co-exist with others in peace and harmony. It is a rare religious tradition of peace and harmony blessed with Lord Buddha's sublime teachings.

Buddhism spread not only at home, but abroad as well. The principles of peace, sympathy, compassion, and charity have formed the lives of innumerable saints and I am proud to say that the declared foreign policy of India is based on *panshasila*, a Buddhist term.

Lord Buddha taught the world that hatred is to be eradicated, not through hatred but by love and compassion. The ultimate goal of Buddhism is to attain the permanent and absolute peace that is Nirvana. This cultivates the culture of tolerance, nonviolence, and selfless service to others. His message and teachings of peace and harmony were so astonishing and powerful that the tyrant conqueror Ashoka was transformed into a peaceful ruler, who not only established peace in his own realm, but entrusted his son Rahula and daughter Sanghamitta to spread the message of peace and harmony to different countries.

Buddhism seeks harmony between self and others and avoidance of any conflict. The basic tenets of Buddhism are to promote peace and harmony within different communities, ethnic and racial groups, and religions. Its specialty is to provide an easy way to understand the ethical code and method of instruction.

The very edicts of nonviolence imply an idea of peace around the world and in the changed modern days' fragmented world, the messages of Lord Buddha hold great relevance, particularly in the prevailing critical juncture when the world is in dire need of peace and harmony. Buddhism has a great role in establishing embedded peace. Therefore, we Buddhists should bear responsibility to inculcate in the human mind the true objective of human life, that is, to maintain *ahimsa*, compassion, love. The core of Buddhism is the Noble Eightfold Path that has been evolved to bring happiness, peace, and harmony, not only for an individual or for a community, but for the world.

The Buddhist ideal of peace is quite clearly defined in the Saddharmapundarika Sutra or the Lotus of the True Law which describes an ethical way of the Bodhisattva that is a life for rendering benefits for mankind and leading to ultimate peace.

Wherever Buddhism spread, it changed the way of organizing communities. It made important changes in the social hierarchy, created opportunities for women, and gave individuals of all classes a role in spiritual practice.

Therefore, the message and principles of Buddhism have attained great significance as far as maintenance of global peace and harmony for mankind is concerned manifesting their reliance on the path of beliefs as taught by Lord Buddha.

It is amply clear that right from the days of Lord Buddha to modern times, the philosophy of Buddhism is doing yeomen service for the entire human race. For example, it can be mentioned that Sakyong Mipham Rinpoche, head priest of the Shambhala lineage, has from time to time held peace conferences in different parts of the world to bring peace, happiness, compassion, and harmony to the people.

We can say that Lord Buddha's noble teachings of defeating the evils and consequently achieving peace have immense impact on the overall well-being of humans, both at home and abroad. This in turn can bring about much-needed universal peace, amity, and harmony. These are imperative to promote peaceful co-existence and relations between countries in modern times when the world is disturbed for one or the other avoidable reasons. We can rightly conclude that we can make our lives sublime by resonating Lord Buddha's eternal words: "With our thoughts, we make the world."

REFERENCES

* *Brainwave: A Multidisciplinary Journal* ,Vol 1, vol 2, vol 3, vol 4, vol 5.

* Brammachary, Pandit Silananda. 2011. *Mahasanti Mahaprem*. Kolkata: Maha Bodhi Book   Agency.

* Mahasthavir, Pandit Dharmadar. 1994. *Dhammapada*, Dharmadhar Bouddha Grantha Prakasani, Calcutta-15.

- Priya, Buddha Mahathero. 2018. *The Light of Peace,* Mahabodhi Book Agency.

- Tagore, Rabindranathi. 1984. *Maitri Bhavana O Bauddha Darshan*. Shantiniketan, India: Visva Bharati University.

- Vivekananda, Swami. 1996. *Buddha O Bauddha Dharma*, 8th ed. West Bengal, India: Belur Math.

- Sankrityayan, Mahapandita Rahul. 1989, Buddhist Philosophy. Moscow: Lenin University.

THE WISDOM OF BUDDHISM FOR WORLD PEACE

Utpal Kanti Chowdhury

President, RBSKS, Kolkata, India

*P*eace is a divine state of happiness in the mind. It is desired by all kinds of people ranging from healthy persons to sick persons, rich to poor, and powerful figures to the wretched. People go to places from mountainous terrains to seashores, from holy shrines to solitary forests in search of peace. But who will give us peace? How shall we achieve it? It is most sought after, most precious, but is the most elusive thing in everybody's life, at home as well as in the international arena.

While taking note of the international situation, I refer to the stirred-up enmity and hatred between Ukraine and Russia, China and Taiwan, Turkey, and Syria, America, and Cuba, India, and its neighboring counties, and so on. The conflicts among them have cast a negative effect on the whole world both politically and economically. Prices of commodities are shooting up causing burn-holes in the pockets of the common people, consequently affecting their private and social lives. The overall situation is destroying the peace and tranquility of both offenders and victims. Tensions are growing everywhere due to direct and indirect reasons and the people in our surroundings and other parts of the globe are desperately seeking emotional support from something or somebody or from some spiritual idea. Here comes the role of Buddhism to bring forth world peace.

Buddhism promotes the idea of world peace through its teachings and practices. The core principles of Buddhism, such as compassion, nonviolence, and mindfulness provide a foundation for cultivating inner peace, which can then extend to promoting peace in the world.

Here are some ways in which Buddhism contributes to the aspiration for world peace:

Compassion and loving-kindness: Buddhism emphasizes the cultivation of compassion and loving-kindness towards all beings. By developing empathy and understanding, Buddhists strive to alleviate suffering and promote harmony among individuals and communities.

Nonviolence: Buddhism advocates nonviolence as a fundamental principle. The first precept in Buddhism is to refrain from harming living beings. This includes not only physical harm but also verbal and mental harm. By adhering to nonviolence, Buddhists work towards resolving conflicts peacefully and fostering a peaceful society.

Interconnectedness and interdependence: Buddhism teaches that all beings are interconnected and interdependent. This concept highlights the idea that everything arises due to multiple causes and conditions. Understanding this interconnectedness encourages Buddhists to recognize the shared humanity and work towards the well-being of all, which can contribute to global harmony.

Mindfulness and Meditation: Buddhism puts significant emphasis on mindfulness and meditation practices. By cultivating awareness and non-reactivity, individuals can develop inner peace and reduce the tendencies towards aggression and violence. This personal transformation can have a ripple effect, leading to more peaceful interactions in society.

Engaged Buddhism: Engaged Buddhism is a contemporary movement within Buddhism that encourages active participation in social and political issues to alleviate suffering and promote peace. Engaged Buddhists apply Buddhist principles and practices to address social injustices, poverty, environmental concerns, and other pressing global challenges.

Dialogue and reconciliation: Buddhism promotes dialogue and reconciliation as a means to resolve conflicts and build understanding. The practice of deep listening, compassionate communication, and forgiveness can contribute to healing personal and collective wounds, thereby fostering peace.

It is important to note that while Buddhism provides valuable insights and tools for promoting peace, achieving world peace requires collective effort from individuals, communities, and societies. Buddhism serves as a guiding philosophy that inspires individuals to work towards peace in their own lives and percolate the same in other people's lives.

Buddhism is not merely a religion of faith and practice, but is a time-tested scientific religion based on spiritual enlightenment and dialectical reasoning. Buddhist philosophy is far more relevant on our crisis-torn world today for establishing world peace on a permanent basis. Buddhism is an outstanding religious theological tradition of peace and harmony. It is based on the philosophy of philanthropic humanism and universal fraternity. This is the hallmark of Lord Buddha's teachings.

REFERENCES

- Brammachary, Pandit Silananda. 2011. *Mahasanti Mahaprem*. Kolkata: Maha Bodhi Book Agency.

- Das, Asha. 2016. Bauddha Darshan O Rabindranath. India: Calcutta University.

- Mahasthavir, Pandit Dharmadar. 1994. *Dhammapada*, Dharmadhar Bouddha Grantha Prakasani, Calcutta.

- Priya, Buddha Mahathero, 2016, *The Light of Peace,* 2nd ed. SUSWM, Kolkata.

- Sen, Ranabrata, ed. 1968. *Dhammapada*, Haraf Prakasani, Kolkata.

- Tagore, Rabindranathi. 1984. *Maitri Bhavana O Bauddha Darshan*. Shantiniketan, India: Visva Bharati University.

- Vivekananda, Swami. 1996. *Buddha O Bauddha Dharma,* 8th ed.. West Bengal, India: Belur Math.

BUDDHISM AND WORLD PEACE

Nima Wangdi Sherpa

*Chairman, Sherpa Development Board and Peace Worker,
Darjeeling*

am honored to speak on behalf of the Sherpa community of Darjeeling about the Nyingmapa tradition of Buddhism. As you may know, the Sherpa community has a long-standing connection with Buddhism, and the Nyingmapa tradition holds a special place in our hearts.

The Nyingmapa tradition of Buddhism is one of the oldest schools of Tibetan Buddhism, and it has a rich history and deep roots in the Himalayan region. The word "Nyingma" means "ancient," and this tradition is known for its emphasis on the teachings of Padmasambhava, also known as Guru Rinpoche, who is considered to be the founder of the Nyingmapa tradition.

The Nyingmapa tradition is characterized by its focus on Dzogchen, or "great perfection," which is a path to enlightenment that emphasizes the innate nature of the mind. This tradition also places great importance on the practice of meditation, which is seen as a means of attaining spiritual realization and liberation.

The Nyingmapa tradition has had a significant impact on the Sherpa community of Darjeeling. Many Sherpas are devoted followers of this tradition, and it has played a central role in our cultural and spiritual practices. The Sherpa community has a long history of serving as guides and porters for mountaineering expeditions in the Himalayas, and our deep connection to Buddhism has helped us to develop a sense of compassion and service to others.

In recent years, the Nyingmapa tradition has faced challenges and disruptions, particularly in Tibet, where there has been political and social upheaval. However, the tradition has persevered, and it continues to have a strong presence in the Himalayan region and beyond.

As members of the Sherpa community, we are proud to be associated with the Nyingmapa tradition of Buddhism. We believe that its teachings have much to offer the world, particularly in a time when there is so much uncertainty and upheaval. We hope that the tradition will continue to thrive and that its message of compassion, wisdom, and spiritual realization will reach more and more people around the world.

In conclusion, I would like to thank you for giving me the opportunity to speak about the Nyingmapa tradition of Buddhism on behalf of the Sherpa community of Darjeeling. We are proud of our connection to this ancient and profound tradition, and we hope that its teachings will continue to inspire and guide us in the years to come.

REFERENCES

- *Brainwave: A Multidisciplinary Journal*, Vols. 1–5.

THE PERSON AND THE COMMUNITY IN EARLY BUDDHISM

Dr. Surajit Barua

Assistant Professor, Seth Anandaram Jaypuriya College, Kolkata

Introduction

*F*or more than 2,500 years, Buddhism has enchanted thinkers and laity alike with its deep insights into the nature of our lived experience and for providing a general, easy, and practical solution to the most fundamental, universal problem plaguing all of humanity since time immemorial.

In this article, I analyze the early Buddhist (Theravada) perspective on the nature of the relation between the person and the community and institutions around them. The first section deals with a brief mention of the two fundamental Buddhist doctrines which underlie all discussions on cultivation of virtue: *paṭiccasamuppāda* and *trilakshana*. In the second section, I describe how the Buddha has given prime importance to building a personal virtuous psychology for embarking on the noble path to Nibbana and how this has led to the notion that Buddhism is individualistic. The third section clarifies the notion of detachment or renunciation and argues that the Buddhist's stance does not preclude social isolation of the Nibbana seeker. The fourth section then cites several instances from the suttas as evidence for the Buddhist's commitment to social service. In the fifth section, I argue that the early Buddhist gives priority to the development of virtuous character of the person rather than performance of virtuous acts. The somewhat lengthy sixth section then argues that the early Buddhists did not recommend direct social or political activism as a means to community welfare. The last section sums up the conclusion.

Paṭiccasamuppāda and Trilaksana

The law of dependent origination implies that any given thing is causally dependent in a given instant on innumerable other entities. Dependence can be on the "cause" side as well as on the "effect" side. A cause of A is, at the same time, an effect of some B. Moreover, there are multiple causes of any event. That is, the set of things that can be regarded as cause or causal conditions (*hetupaccaya*) of A is not a fixed set. *Paṭiccasamuppāda* is expressed as the twelve links, which make the wheel of becoming (*bhava-cakka*) revolve. The twelve links range over three lives and their arrangement resembles a circle, not a line. Each link is dependent on every other link and together they perpetuate *samsara*, the beginningless cycle of rebirth, dukkha, and dying again. Some form of suffering invariably accompanies existence. For cessation of suffering, breaking the link or cycle is essential. How can one do so? By having knowledge of the true nature of reality (*trilaksana*). Failure to recognize it is *avijja* (ignorance). On the significance of trilakshana in Buddhist teachings, Westerhoff writes: "If it makes sense to speak of a conceptual core of the Buddhist teachings, the trilaksana is probably one of best candidates for inclusion in it."

The following three constitute the basic characteristics of the phenomenal world (*trilakkhana*):

1. All saṅkhāras are impermanent: sabbe saṅkhārā aniccā

2. All saṅkhāras are unsatisfactory: sabbe saṅkhārā dukkhā

3. All dhammas (all things including the unconditioned) are without self: sabbe dhammā anattā

The word *sankhara* has multiple, related meanings. Here, sankhara[56] stands for all conditioned, constructed, and compounded mental, as well as physical things in the universe that are formed as a result of conditioning by preceding causes and conditions.

Let us briefly discuss the three characteristics:

Anicca (The impermanence of sankharas)

Since every sankhara is composed of multiple constituents which are in turn composed of further entities and every such entity is causally affected by innumerable more entities, every conditioned, constructed, and compounded thing is impermanent. Instability and change prevail in all events and entities, in all the mental and material phenomena that have the nature to rise and fall. Thus, *anicca* (impermanence) follows naturally from *pratiyutta samutpada*.

Dukkha (suffering or unsatisfactory nature of sankharas)

In the Dukkhata Sutta of the Samyutta Nikaya,[57] the Buddha described three different levels of suffering:

i. Dukkha dukkha – Refers to suffering due to physical pain

---

56 The five skandhas: form (rupa), feeling (vedana), perception (sanna), mental formations (sankhara) and consciousness (vinnana) which constitute the person or a being, can also be considered as conditioned phenomena (sankhara). As the fourth aggregate of the five aggregates (panchakkhanda), sankhara refers to the mental forces or volitions responsible for bodily and mental activity, for example, hunger, attentiveness, and emotions.

57 Bhikkhu Bodhi, 1999, Dukkhata Sutta (SN 45.165), *The Connected Discourses of the Buddha, A Translation of the Samyutta Nikaya* (Massachusetts: Wisdom Publications).

---

and mental distress resulting from birth, growing old, illness and dying. This is the common, ordinary sense in which we use the term *dukkha*. Some dukha dukkhas cannot be avoided in the present life because they are a product of the very nature of conditioned existence. Anybody who is born has to endure them. All you can do is to put effort through paññā, sīla, samādhi in this life and extinguish the fires of raga (craving for attachment) which is primarily responsible for bhāva. However, we endure some dukkha dukkhas due to our lack of knowledge about how the cosmos works.

ii. Viparinama dukkha – This refers to suffering due to the impermanent, transient nature of everything that exists. Since nothing has a fixed essence (*swabhava*) and is transient, nothing has the capacity to consistently and stably provide pleasure or pain or indifference. Cessation of this type of suffering lies in the knowledge that no event or entity is inherently good or bad. There is no point in trying to avoid or hate change or impermanence. The sooner I accept *anicca* as the fundamental nature of every *sankhara,* the sooner the *klesa* (mental defilement) of aversion (*dvesa*) gets erased. When the *avarana* of *dvesa* is removed, I stop complaining "why me?" I realize that every event, whatever its impact on us is merely a conditioned event which happened due to the presence of its conditioning causes and not because it wanted me to suffer or because I am unlucky.

iii. Sankhara dukkha –This is the most subtle form of dukkha which points to a basic all-pervasive dissatisfaction that we experience as a result of our conditioned existence. Because of a wrong worldview, we tend to have mental dispositions to prefer certainty over the uncertain, stable over the unstable, fixed over the momentary, one over many, and unity over diversity. Such categorizing preferences, in turn, lead to such cravings whose fulfilments are incompatible with the consequences following from the law of dependent origination. Such mental fabrication or conceptualization is called *papañca*. Our tendency to "judge" someone or stereotype a community on the basis of insufficient evidence are obvious examples.

Papañca leads to delusion and confusion (*moha*) in us. Moha leads us to doubt our own rational faculties in our attempts to discover truths. Consequently, we become prone to misleading information, rumors and we become restless. The starting point to eradicating sankhara dukkha is therefore, to cultivate the mental state of *sati*. In the Satipaṭṭhāna Sutta the term *sati* means to maintain awareness of reality, whereby the true nature of phenomena can be seen.[58] In modern parlance, it can be loosely translated as mindfulness though it is not just bare attention.

Anatta (no-self)

The common view is that the self is the essence of a person. The denotation of the word "I," whose continued existence is supposed to be necessary for the person to exist. Alternatively, one can think of "I" (or "you" or any proper name) as merely a name conventionally referring merely to the unique but impermanent arrangement of all the parts (*skandhas*) of the person collectively-nothing more, nothing less. The person is nothing more than a complex of five transient aggregates (*skandhas*)[59]. If we combine this view with the Buddhist doctrine of *anicca,* the result is the view that there is no essence of a person that can be said to exist beyond one moment. In other words, there is no self. Belief in the existence of a soul, *satkāyadṛṣṭi* is the root cause of our notion of I-ness, and consequently of our own sufferings. The assumption of a stable driver soul is not necessary to explain the unity of experience and cohesiveness in thought and activity of the person.

Just as impermanence (anicca) follows from pratiyutya samutpada, anatta follows from anicca. If everything is impermanent and is conditioned, at any given moment, by innumerable factors, then it cannot have a fixed essence. The appearance of a continuously existing, same person across many moments is

---

58 Robert Sharf, "Mindfulness and Mindlessness in Early Chan," *Philosophy East and West,* October 2014.

59 The simile of the chariot from the Milindapanha, a text from the second century BCE, regarding answers of the King Menander, a Greek who ruled northwestern India, by a Buddhist monk Nagasena, is often quoted to support this point.

illusory. The illusion may be compared to the flame of a lamp. The name "flame" does not have a fixed referent; the constituents of the flame change every moment and yet we conventionally refer to the ever-changing diverse constituents of the name by a single name. The so-called self of the person is likewise an "empty" concept of everyday usage.

Our bondage in samsara (and the consequent three types of suffering) is a result of the wrong view (on how to achieve salvation) due to the absence of knowledge (*avijja*) of the above three *laksanas*.

The Significance of the Person in Early Buddhism

In his first teaching after enlightenment, encoded in the Dhammacakkappavattana Sutta, the Buddha preached avoidance of both the mutually opposing extreme positions of self-indulgence and self-mortification. In a later teaching, the Kaccayanagotta Sutta, the Buddha described the *majjhimapaṭipadā* (the middle way view) as denying both the extremes of eternalism (some things are permanently existing) and annihilationism (the body changes or gets destroyed). The middle way is to follow the Noble Eightfold Path. The eight factors of the path are traditionally divided into three parts: moral virtue (*sīla*) comprised of three factors: right speech, right action, and right livelihood; right effort, right mindfulness, and right concentration constitute mental concentration (*samādhi)*, and wisdom (*paññā*) comprises the remaining factors: right view and right thought. Out of the eight factors, the Mahā Cattārīsaka Sutta clearly establishes the primacy of the right view (*sammā-diṭṭhi*). The right view is to adopt the middle way; the wrong view is to think in binaries. Binary thinking is the tendency to see things in terms of mutually exclusive absolutes. For example, to think that the self exists either permanently or does not exist at all is binary thinking. Similarly, to think that a good life consists in either indulgence in immediate sensual pleasure or total suppression of sensual needs (through self-mortification) is binary too.

Unfortunately, over time some scholars and new branches of Buddhism have applied binary thinking to the principles of early

Buddhism to make extreme conclusions. The fact that Theravada holds the person solely responsible for his salvation has been given a dichotomous, binary interpretation to mean that it seeks *only* personal emancipation *at the cost of* community welfare.[60] Dipen Barua observes:[61]

The idea of a "self-centered" path arose as a polemical strategy devised by the emergent Mahayana tradition nearly two millennia ago. The new Vehicle needed to defend itself from claims of inauthenticity or heresy, and Mahayana writers formed a sophisticated body of apologetics to counter detractors, from new exegetical methods to a broader hermeneutics of scriptural insight and revelation. Another strategy was the "Mahayana-Hinayana" distinction, which notably is used today only by Mahayana and Vajrayana practitioners and is not used in Theravada.

If we examine the notion of detachment in early Buddhism closely, it becomes clear that such allegations cannot be sustained.

Buddha on Detachment

In the Anguttara Nikaya, the Buddha explains and advocates the advantages of renunciation: "May I have nothing to do with fame, Nāgita, nor may fame come upon me! Whosoever cannot obtain at will, easily and without difficulty, this happiness of renunciation, this happiness of seclusion, this happiness of peace, this happiness of enlightenment as I obtain it, let him enjoy this filthy and slothful happiness, this happiness gotten of gains, homage, and publicity."[62]

Note that the contrast in the above passage is between happiness sought from renunciation, seclusion, peace, and enlightenment on

---

60 For an excellent survey, see Donna Lynn Brown, "Is Buddhism Individualistic? The Trouble with a Term." *Journal of Buddhist Ethics*, 2021.
61 Dipen Barua "Self and Other: Practicing Welfare for Individual and Community." Available online at BuddhistDoor.net. Accessed on 6/28/23, https://www.buddhistdoor.net/features/self-and-other-practicing-welfare-for-individual-and-community/
62 Nyanaponika Thera and Bhikkhu Bodhi, trans. (2008). Aṅguttara Nikāya Anthology Part II (urbandharma.org), accessed on 5/30/23, https://www.urbandharma.org/pdf1/wh208AnguttaraNikaya2.pdf .

one hand and that sought from gains, homage, and publicity on the other. Thus, renunciation or seclusion should be interpreted as detachment from (or avoidance of) craving for: (i) material gains, and (ii) immaterial gains: (a) merit from homage and (b) fame. This is not an injunction against one's social commitments which are of the nature of duty.

The Buddha never supported extreme ascetic withdrawal as that could mean depriving the body and the mind of its normal nourishments. Such practices can lead to repression of craving rather than purging mental defilements once and for all. Elizabeth Harris remarks: "The detachment of which Buddhism speaks, therefore, is not an extreme turning away from that which normally nourishes the human body. Neither is it a closing of the eyes to all beauty."[63]

A person earns merit (punya) only when he acts with intentions which manifest his concern for the welfare of others. Someone who locks himself away in isolation with the aim of Nibbana is only getting farther from it. Such a person regards other persons and the community as obstructions on his path to Nibbana. In thinking of the other as his adversary, he affirms a unique essence (*swabhav*) for himself by implication. Moreover, as humans we have several physiological needs for nourishment which must be met. Likewise, social withdrawal deprives oneself[64] of the mental need of longingness with other humans. Thus, physical withdrawal can be the product of both selfishness and intention of deliberate suffering.

The kind of renunciation the Buddha advocates is that which brings about the absence of craving/raga (i.e., *virāga*). It denotes non-attachment to the four types of objects of grasping: sense pleasures (*kamupadana*), views (*ditthupadana*), rules and customs (*silabbatupadana*) and a belief in the continued self, different

---

63 Elizabeth J. Harris (1997). *Detachment and Compassion in Early Buddhism*. Sri Lanka: Buddhist Publication Society,   https://www.accesstoinsight.org/lib/authors/harris/bl141.html
64 Here, the use of the word "self" is in the mundane, conventional sense.

from the five skandhas (*attavadupadana*). It is this dispassionate distancing and lack of interest in grasping (appropriation) of the four types of objects that is preferred in Buddhist renunciation.

The Early Buddhist View on Moral Duty to the Other

One is actually encouraged to fulfil his worldly obligations. The Anguttara Nikāya, along with the Sīgalaka Sutta in the Digha Nikāya, are replete with Buddha's guidance on the householder's responsibilities towards his family members and the society at large. Bhikkhu Bodhi remarks: "He set up a pragmatic but inspiring ideal for the laity, that of the *sappurisa* or "good person," who lives "for the good, welfare, and happiness of many people," his parents, his wife and children, the domestic help, his friends, and contemplative renouncers (AN 5.42). In offering guidance to the family, the Buddha prescribes the duties of children towards their parents (AN 2.33, AN 3.31), advises husbands and wives how to live together (AN 4.53), and even instructs a loving couple how they can be assured of reuniting in future lives (AN 4.5)."[65]

Lily DeSilva adds:

In the Anguttara Nikaya the Buddha describes, with sacrificial terminology, three types of fires that should be tended with care and honor (A.iv, 44). They are *ahuneyyaggi, gahapataggi,* and *dakkhineyyaggi*. The Buddha explained that *ahuneyyaggi* means one's parents, and they should be honored and cared for. *Gahapataggi* means one's wife and children, employees, and dependents. *Dakkineyyaggi* represents religious persons who have either attained the goal of arahantship or have embarked on a course of training for the elimination of negative mental traits. All these should be cared for and looked after as one would tend a sacrificial fire. According to the Mahamangala Sutta, offering hospitality to one's relatives is one of the great auspicious deeds a layperson can perform (SN. 262–63).[11]

There are ten wholesome/meritorious deeds (dasa kusala kamma) and ten unwholesome/immoral deeds (*dasa akusala*

---

65 Bhikkhu Bodhi. 2012. *A Thematic Guide to the Aṅguttara Nikāya*, https://suttacentral.net/?lang=en

kamma). The immorality *(akusalata)* of the unwholesome deeds follows from their potential to harm or hurt (psychologically, physically, or verbally) the other (including nonhumans). Likewise, the wholesomeness of the kusala kamma comes from their potential to alleviate the suffering of the other. Thus, what is good/bad for the salvation-striver is good/bad for the community too.[12]

Virtuous Acts or Virtuous Mind?

However, there is something very important about Buddhist ethics which must be stressed. In Charles Goodman's words: "The Buddhist technical terms we might be inclined to translate as "virtuous" (such as the Pali *kusala*) are, in the first instance, applied to occurrent mental states."[66] That is, it is not the action itself which determines its *kusalata* or *akusalata*. Rather, it is the intention behind the voluntary action which determines its merit. In the Anguttara Nikaya (AN), the Buddha says, "It is *cetana* (intention or volition) that I call kamma" (AN III 415). Richard Gombrich observes: "It is intention that I call karma" is the Buddha's answer to brahmin ritualism. The focus of interest shifted from physical action, involving people and objects in the real world, to psychological process."[67,68]

Principles of right moral conduct, expressed in terms of moral duties or rules known as precepts, are as much codes of conduct

---

66 [11]Bhikkhu Bodhi, *The Connected Discourses of the Buddha: A New Translation of the Samyutta Nikaya* (Massachusetts: Wisdom Publications, 2000).

[12] Charles Goodman. (2009). *Consequences of Compassion: An Interpretation and Defense of Buddhist Ethics*. (Oxford: Oxford University Press, 2009), 195.
131

67 R. F, Gombrich. *How Buddhism Began: The Conditioned Genesis of the Early Teachings* (New York: Routledge, 2006), 51.
68 However, the Puññakiriyavatthusutta (A 8.1) mentions three bases of meritorious deeds (Kusalakamma): giving (dāna), moral virtue (sīla) and mental cultivation (bhāvanā). Psychological development comes third, presumably in terms of importance and moreover, there is no mention of wisdom as a base. This, however, doesn't contradict the above claim for the three grounds of merit-making are a training model for the laity and for non-contemplative monastics.

for psychological development as they are foundations of creating a just and harmonious society. Several such sets of precepts (e.g., *pañcaśīla, aṣṭāṅga,* and *daśa, śīla*) are mentioned in the sutras for both the laity and the monks. They are to be followed because any virtuous person who has successfully counteracted negative dispositions called *kleśas* or vices (and has therefore prepared himself for Nirvana) would internalize them as beliefs and apply them naturally and spontaneously through their conduct with others and the environment. The Sonadanda Sutta too emphasizes the complimentary, reinforcing nature of personal wisdom-a private pursuit on one hand and morality-our duty to others in the community-on the other: "Ethics and wisdom always go together. An ethical person is wise, and a wise person ethical. And ethics and wisdom are said to be the best things in the world. It's just like when you clean one hand with the other, or clean one foot with the other."[69]

Even when the Buddha advises public administrators on how to govern, the focus is not on how they should control their subjects into submission. The emphasis rather is on personal conduct and thought. Kuddaka Nikāya and Jātaka tales specify ten duties (*dasavidha rājadhamma*) that kings and administrators should follow: charity, morality, altruism, honesty, gentleness, self-control, non-anger, nonviolence, forbearance, and uprightness (*danamsilampariccagam, ajjavammaddavamtapam; akkodhamavihimsanca, khantincaavirodhanam*). Thus, the path to social welfare starts with each person's psychological purification. Compassion (*karunā*) is one of the four sublime states (*brahma vihāras*), the other states being goodwill (*mettā*), sympathetic joy (*muditā*), and equanimity (*upekkhā*). A Nibbana seeker is supposed to cultivate these states in meditation in order to cleanse the mind of the defilements (*kleshas rāga, dvesa* and *moha*) and prepare it for right concentration (*sammā samādhi*).

It is understandable why the Buddha placed greater emphasis

---

69 *Digha Nikaya*, Bhikkhu Sujato, trans. 2018 (Soṇadaṇḍa Sutta) suttacentral.net accessed on 5/29/23.

on cultivating unlimited goodwill before the actual performance of an act of compassion. An act of love or compassion may be a form of asserting power or control over the other. It may be a medium or strategy for imposing an ideology or culture on the beneficiary. An act of altruism may be backed by a bad intention following from mental defilements or it may be a product of a duty borne out of one's commitment or duty towards the particular community to which he is affiliated. Wrong intention for helping others would be, for instance, the desire for fame or protection or favor or a good image in society. It may even follow from a false sense of belongingness (mine) to a particular community. For example, you might feel obliged to help X (but not Y) because X belongs to your community. Bad intentions may work even at a subtle level, making us think and act in ways which bring suffering. For example, buoyed by a false sense of supremacy (of self or that of one's own community), the imperialist invaders often systematically destroyed ancient forms of knowledge in the colonies in the name of making the natives "civilized." Similarly, in some families, influential members force others in the family to make choices which may not be conducive to their flourishing, however good the underlying motive may be. The point is help may be given where it is not required. Even with the right intentions, acts of altruism and social or political activism may be misinterpreted.

For true acts of altruism, one has to propagate the Dhamma to individual persons. This is the greatest form of altruism, for it is these reformed individuals with the right view who would go on to construct better, egalitarian societies whose rules, customs, and rituals would benefit all. That is perhaps why the focus is on building the right state of mind through *prāgya, silā* and *samādhi.* A compassionate mind having unlimited goodwill, purged of defilements, drives one to act spontaneously with pure altruistic intention, expecting nothing for the self (no-self) in return for the favor done.

The Early Buddhist on Social and Political Activism

Some later Buddhists and even some contemporary followers

advocate the reverse approach. They emphasize the significance of social involvement for moral upliftment. Socially engaged Buddhists think that practicing Buddhism necessarily involves social and political activism. Patricia Hunt-Perry and Lyn Fine[70] ascribe the following quote to Thich Nhat Hanh, the originator of the Engaged Buddhism movement: "Buddhism is already engaged Buddhism. If it is not, it is not Buddhism.'That is, to participate actively involved in social and political affairs and work for systemic change is a moral obligation for the Buddhist."

Note, however, that in the textual evidence cited above, the recommended altruistic and social responsibility is directed from persons to persons .On the contrary, there are several recorded instances wherein the Buddha refused to be drawn into social or political disputes involving communities or ideologies. For example, he was initially reluctant in admitting women into the Sangha. He agreed only after laying down eight rules (*garudhammas*) for bhikkhuni ordination, in addition to the 227 rules of monastic discipline, the Vinaya which all bhikkhus have to follow. Another restriction imposed on female followers is that married women had to seek the permission of both the parents and the husbands for ordination, but no such restriction was formulated for married men.[71] Thus, it is clear that he did not challenge or plan to overthrow the existing social order. There are more such instances stated below.

One should not apply binary thinking here and construe from his silence on community issues that he tacitly approved of discriminatory social practices. That he did not is clear from the way he constituted and ran his monastic order, whose administration was based on democratic principles, and which did not discriminate amongst its inhabitants based on their birth. Casteism was prevalent and democracy was absent in the community, outside the Sangha and yet the Buddha chose to tread

70 Patricia Hunt-Perry and Lyn Fine. "All Buddhism Is Engaged: Thich Nhat Hanh and the Order of Interbeing." In *Engaged Buddhism in the West*, edited by Christopher S. Queen (Massachussetts: Wisdom Publications, 2000), 35–66.
71 V. Pandita, "Did the Buddha Correct Himself?" *Journal of Buddhist Ethics* (2014), 474.

a different path within the monastic order. Why then did he follow the patriarchy and impose restrictions on his female followers who wished to join as bhikkhunis? What explains the difference in approach? I think a possible explanation is that dissatisfaction against the all-pervading authority of the Vedas and its ritual-centric ethics was already simmering in the society by the time the Buddha started propagating his dhamma. Thus, he could reject casteism while formulating monastic rules without inviting violent backlashes from the monarchy or the general public. In contrast, the patriarchy was deep-rooted in the society and challenging it with radical moves might have invited the wrath of the powers-that-be. Violent obstruction could have harmed all his disciples and slowed down the propagation of the Dhamma. That is probably why he imposed additional restrictions on the ordination of women. These restrictions were deliberately not strong enough to deter the motivated; they were just enough to steer clear of trouble. The purportedly firsthand accounts of bhikkhunis in the Therigatha prove that the women within the Sangha were far better treated than they were outside, and they felt emancipated. Thus, the restrictive rules were effective more in letter than in spirit.

Amod Lele gives several examples from classical Indian Buddhist texts to show that early Buddhism discouraged active participation in political and social affairs:

The Rajja Sutta (SN I.116–117) goes yet further. Here, even to rule according to dharma (*dhammena*) is presented to the Buddha as a *temptation from Māra*, the evil tempter figure. As the Buddha comes closer to awakening, he wonders: "Is it possible to exercise rulership righteously [*dhammena*] without killing and without instigating others to kill, without confiscating and without instigating others to confiscate, without borrowing and without causing sorrow?" Māra replies that he can and should indeed rule righteously. But the Buddha, of course, refuses this temptation, and proceeds instead on the monastic path.[72]

---

72 Amod Lele, "Disengaged Buddhism," *Journal of Buddhist Ethics* 26 (2019), 256–257..

In the Gilāna Sutta (SN IV. 302–304), the highly regarded householder disciple Citta is sick and about to die, and the gods ask him to vow that he will become a *cakravartin*. But he turns them down, saying: "That too is impermanent; that too is unstable; one must abandon that too and pass on." Citta is not a bodhisattva or aspiring to be a buddha; he is simply aiming at arhatship, the lower kind of awakening possible for a normal person. But even that is a greater goal than being a ruler who will bring general prosperity and flourishing to his society.[73]

The Buddha's silence is even more striking in the Mahāparinibbāna Sutta where King Ajātasattu's minister requested his opinion on the king's plan to invade and wipe out the Vajjis. In response, the Buddha only specified seven factors: *sattaaparihāniyā dhamma* which, if followed, would ensure growth and prevent decline of the community of the Vajjis. But he did not condemn Ajātasattu's decision to indulge in violence and destruction. This seemed odd to some scholars (e.g., Damien Keown 2020) because in such situations, one would expect the Buddha to vehemently discourage all violent political actions as they undermine the dignity of the person.

What could be the reason for such accounts of political disengagement in early Buddhist texts? The Cakkavatti Sīhanāda Sutta provides the clue. It begins and ends with the following passage:

Monks, be islands unto yourselves, be a refuge unto yourselves with no other refuge. Let the Dhamma be your island, let the Dhamma be your refuge, with no other refuge. . .. Keep to your own preserves, monks, to your ancestral haunts. If you do so, then Māra will find no lodgement, no foothold. It is just by the building-up of wholesome states that this merit increases.[74]

In between, the sutta describes a story of how a once-flourishing kingdom spiralled into moral and economic decline and the lives

73 Ibid.
74 Dīgha Nikāya Vol. III, trans. Maurice Walshe (Pali Text Society edition), 58.

of its citizens got worse over time once the king failed to help the needy. At some point, a desperate group of people reach the conclusion: "It is only because we became addicted to evil ways that we suffered this loss of our kindred, so let us now do good! What good things can we do? Let us abstain from the taking of life-that will be a good practice."[75] This moral action improves their lives and feeling encouraged, they undertake other moral activities as well. As a result, gradually, order would return to the community and ultimately, a new Cakravartin will arise, as will the future Buddha Metteyya (Maitreya). In the final lines, the story returns to the present where the Buddha affirms the premise that was stated in the beginning: "Monks, be islands unto yourselves..."

Rejecting objections of inconsistency, Lele and Stevens Collins have rightly noted that the embedded story actually complements the advice to the monks in the beginning and end of the sutra. Lele argues:

Good and bad social systems will come and go, and they will get worse before they get better. So, the narrative provides a reason why the text's audience should build personal virtue and embrace the dharma, *rather than* placing its hope in those social systems or any idea of progress therein . . . moral improvement is what ultimately makes the material conditions better. To do so, the text says, audience members can and should disengage from society. Then they will no longer be dependent on social conditions for their well-being.[76]

I think the above explanation is correct, but it requires elaboration. We may consider all social and political systems as analogous to the games we play.[77] For your actions to be counted as moves within a game of play, you need to follow its constituting rules. These rules may not be perfect, but their validity has to be presupposed if you aspire to be a good player. You can sincerely

---

75   Ibid.,73.
76   Op. cit. Lele, 264.
77   I have borrowed the games analogy from the famous philosopher, Ludwig Wittgenstein.

assess the validity of the rules only from a distance when you are not playing the game. Similarly, any community or institution functions according to some fundamental, constituting rules and beliefs decided by a group of individuals who matter in that community. Any social or political action you do or any idea you propose, which is intended at servicing this community inevitably makes you implicitly, by default, the supporter of the fundamental, constituting beliefs of that institution or community; you will be publicly seen as a defender of those underlying rules, norms and beliefs even if you explicitly deny so. The problem with such a state of affairs is since these institutions are not global and material resources are limited, any act which promotes the stability and welfare of the community might lead to suffering of individuals, within or outside these institutions.

For example, the duty of an army soldier is to serve his nation during war even if that means inflicting suffering on citizens of the enemy country. Similarly, a human resource official is duty bound to transfer an employee to a far-off place in the interest of the company even if that means inflicting suffering on the family of the transferee employee. The obligation to fulfil their respective duties comes from their implicit commitment to essential principles governing the material welfare of their respective institutions. They are justified in their actions if considered from within those institutions. But from a neutral and global perspective, it is plainly wrong to indulge in such activities as they exacerbate the suffering of individual persons. Lele remarks:

The text (Aggañña Sutta) explicitly proclaims that accusation, punishment, and banishment are bad (*pāpaka, akusala*), just as the original thefts are (DN III. 93). Their role in maintaining society does not stop them from creating bad karma and interfering with one's progress to Nirvana. Likewise, in the Mūgapakkha Jātaka, the Bodhisatta (buddha-to-be) is born as a prince whose father rules according to dharma (*dhammena*).Yet even so, when the Bodhisatta sees his father punishing criminals, he thinks, "Ah! my father *through his being* a king, is becoming guilty of a grievous action which brings men to hell."[78]

This explains why the Buddha could have chosen to become a Chakkavatin king and attempted to eradicate suffering using all his state-given powers, but he chose to be a wandering mendicant instead; acting according to the Rajdharma would have obligated him to undertake acts which are against the Dhamma.

Directly attempting to reform the community without reforming the individuals within it might lead to rejecting the fundamental community beliefs, only to be replaced by a new set of community beliefs which are fundamental to the newly formed community. But some of these new beliefs could again be against the Dhamma because they might not be conducive to the welfare of *all* beings in the cosmos. So, it makes sense to reform the individual first, irrespective of his affiliations. That is why the Buddha neither advised Ajātasattu against invasion nor did he protest against the prevalent patriarchy in the then society. It would not only be futile but the disfavor from the powers-that-be might bring to the Sangha would have impeded the spread of the Dhamma, which is the vehicle through which real welfare for all beings can be achieved.

Conclusion

For the Buddhist, the individual person is not simply a cog in the giant wheel of samsara. He has the capacity to break free from the never-ending cycle of births and rebirths through his own actions following from right intentions. He does not need anyone's blessings or pay obeisance to the "ultimate power" to end his sufferings; Worship of the Buddha or his idol by his followers is merely out of veneration; it is not a means to salvation. By decentralizing the power of salvation and distributing it among the masses, the Buddha empowered the person. All are born equal (in the sense that everybody is subject to conditional existence) and anybody can become the Buddha by conducting himself in harmony with the true nature of reality, just as Gautama Buddha did.

In this journey of emancipation, the person has to first purge

---

78   Ibid., 265–256.

the defilements of his mind which have arisen due to lack of knowledge about the true nature of reality. Through right conduct and right concentration on his subconscious psychological activity and wisdom, he can build a character and dispositions that are conducive to attaining Nibbana. The conditionality of all phenomena makes it imperative for the right view and character to entail a cosmopolitan, egalitarian, and compassionate attitude towards all beings.

Early Buddhism doesn't prescribe rules for the conduct of local communities or institutions because every local community is based on some constitutive rules which are based on local concerns. Thus, they fail to incorporate the possibility of welfare for all beings which is the essence of the Dhamma. For this reason, the Buddha refrains from supporting any one form of ideology or institution. Rather, once the ruler or a group of persons develops a virtuous character according to the Dhamma, they are in a position to formulate rules for the community which are conducive to the welfare of all and also satisfy the situational needs of its members.

REFERENCES

- Barua, Dipen. "Self and Other: Practicing Welfare for Individual and Community." Available   o n l i n e at BuddhistDoor.net, accessed 6/28/23,   https://www.buddhistdoor.net/features/self-and-other-practicing-welfare-for-   individual-and-community/

- Bodhi, Bhikkhu. *A Thematic Guide to the Aṅguttara Nikāya*, accessed 8/14/23, https://suttacentral.net/an-introduction-bodhi?lang=en

- Bodhi, Bhikkhu. *The Connected Discourses of the Buddha, A Translation of the Samyutta   N i k a y a .* Massachusetts: Wisdom Publications, 1999.

- Bodhi, Bhikkhu. *The Connected Discourses of the Buddha: A New Translation of the Samyutta N i k a y a .*

Massachusetts: Wisdom Publications, 2000.

- Bodhi, Bhikkhu. *Dukkhata Sutta* (SN 45.165). *The Connected Discourses of the Buddha, A Translation of the Samyutta Nikaya*, Massachusetts: Wisdom Publications, 1999.

- Carpenter, J.E., ed. *Dīgha Nikāya, Volume III*. (1910, 1992, corrected reprint 2006) Pali Text Society edition. Translation: Walshe.

- Davids, T. William Rhys. *Milinda Panha*. Google Books. Accessed August 10, 2023,

- https://www.google.com/books/edition/The_Milinda_Panha/tdT1Lne0hSkC?hl=en&gbpv=1&pg=PT2&printsec=frontcover

- Gombrich, R.F. *How Buddhism Began: The Conditioned Genesis of the Early Teachings*. New York: Routledge, 2006.

- Goodman, Charles. *Consequences of Compassion: An Interpretation and Defense of Buddhist Ethics*. Oxford: Oxford University Press, 2009.

- Harris, Elizabeth. *Detachment and Compassion in Early Buddhism*. Sri Lanka: Buddhist Publication Society, accessed 8/14/23, https://www.accesstoinsight.org/lib/authors/harris/bl141.html

- Hunt-Perry, Patricia and Fine, Lyn. "All Buddhism Is Engaged: Thich Nhat Hanh and the Order of Interbeing," in *Engaged Buddhism in the West*, edited by Christopher S. Queen (Massachussetts: Wisdom Publications, 2000, 35–66.

- Lele, Amod. "Disengaged Buddhism." *Journal of Buddhist Ethics* 26 (2019), 256–257.

- Nyanaponika, Thera and Bodhi, Bhikkhu, trans. *Aṅguttara Nikāya Anthology Part II*. (urbandharma.org) 2008. Accessed 5/30/23, https://www.urbandharma.org/pdf1/

wh208AnguttaraNikaya2.pdf

- Pandita, V. "Did the Buddha Correct Himself?" *Journal of Buddhist Ethics,* 2014, 474.

- Priya, Buddha Mahathero. 2016, *The Light of Peace*, 2nd ed., SUSWM, Kolkata.

- Sharf, Robert. "Mindfulness and Mindlessness in Early Chan," *Philosophy East and West,*　October 2014.

- Sujato, Bhikkhu, trans. *Digha Nikaya,* 2018 (Soṇadaṇḍa Sutta) suttacentral.net accessed on　5/29/23.

- Walshe, Maurice, trans. *Dīgha Nikāya Vol. III*. Pali Text Society edition.

MY DHAMMA JOURNEY TO SATIPATTHANA

Subroto Barua

President, Shantiniketan Ambedkar Buddhist Welfare Mission,
West Bengal

Working President, Buddha Triratna Mission, New Delhi

Governing Body Member, Mahabodhi Society of India

As the elders say, the entire teaching of Buddha is the art of living and a priceless gift of Dhamma to mankind. If one lives the life of *sila*, of morality, this itself is an art of living. But living an ethical life, while having many negative reactions in the mind, also makes one unhappy. The Buddha teaches that by observing and purifying the mind i.e., samadhi and pañña, along with sila, one lives a very peaceful and harmonious life. When one lives a life of negativity, one remains tense within and gives nothing but tension to others. When one is living a peaceful, harmonious life, one generates peace and harmony for oneself as well as others. It is for this reason we call Buddha's teaching an art of living, a way of life, a code of conduct.

I practice vipasanna continuously daily for one hour in the morning. In my own life before practicing vipassana, I found my personal tensions were so horrible that I remained miserable and I made others miserable. Coming onto the Path, I found that I was much relieved. I started living a better life, which was more beneficial for the members of my family, for my friends and for society. So if an individual remains full of negativity, society suffers. If an individual changes for the better, it has a good effect on society too.

With such feelings of positive changes DoW started organizing an annual one-day Anapana Meditation Workshop called "The Mindful Child" in association with Gautam Buddha University in February 2014. This was our way to introduce children from school and colleges and also adults to learn more about meditation in daily life. We incorporated the anapana meditation program in our monthly Dhamma talk. When we were regularly organizing dhamma talks and anapana meditation, our Dhamma Guru, Ven. Kaccayana Sraman, usually used to say a Satipathanna course is to be done sincerely to understand vipasanna properly. To act on his advice, I procured the Mahasatipatthana Sutta published by VRI in both Hindi and English. For an entire year, I studied this book, but it made no difference to my vipassana practice. Finally, I decided to book my seat for a Satipatthana course at Dhamma Patthana, Kammaspur Village, Sonepat, Haryana from August 2–10, 2015. As is known today, Kammaspur is an important site in the life of the Buddha.

Satipathana Sutta

This Mahasatipatthana Sutta is the great discourse of awareness given by Buddha:

Thus have I heard: At one time the Enlightened One was staying among the Kurus at Kammāsadhamma, a market town of the Kuru people. There the Enlightened One addressed the monks thus: "Monks," and they replied, "Venerable Sir!" Then the Enlightened One spoke.

This is the one and only way, monks, for the purification of beings, for the overcoming of sorrow and lamentation, for the extinguishing of suffering and grief, for walking on the path of truth, for the realisation of Nibbāna: that is to say, the fourfold establishing of awareness.

Which four? Here, monks, a monk dwells ardent with awareness and constant thorough understanding of impermanence, observing body in body, having removed craving and aversion towards the world (of mind and matter); he dwells ardent with awareness and constant thorough understanding of impermanence, observing sensations in sensations, having removed craving and aversion towards the world [of mind and matter]; he dwells ardent with awareness and constant thorough understanding of impermanence, observing mind in mind, having removed craving and aversion towards the world [of mind and matter]; he dwells ardent with awareness and constant thorough understanding of impermanence, observing mental contents in mental contents, having removed craving and aversion towards the world [of mind and matter.[79]

The Results of the Establishing of Awareness

Indeed, monks, whoever practises this fourfold establishing of awareness in this manner for seven years, he may expect one of two results: in this very life highest wisdom or, if a substratum of aggregates remains, the stage of non-returner.

Let alone seven years, monks. Should any person practise this fourfold establishing of awareness in this manner for six years, one of two results may be expected in him: in this very life highest wisdom or, if a substratum of aggregates remains, the stage of non-returner.[80] *Evaṃ* (in this manner), as explained throughout

---

79 *Mahasatipatthana Sutta*, Vipassana Research Institute (Igatpuri, India). Accessed 8/15/23, https://www.vridhamma.org/node/2786
80 Ibid.

the entire sutta, is *ātāpī sampajāno satimā* (ardent with awareness of mind and body at the level of sensations and with constant thorough understanding of impermanence). In order to achieve these guaranteed results, the continuity should be *sampajaññaṃ na riñcati* (the meditator does not lose the constant thorough understanding of impermanence even for a moment). This is the final stage of liberation of an arahant. The stage of an *anāgāmī* (non-returner) is the third and next-to-last stage of liberation.

In the course at Kammaspura, detailed teachings and practices were taught:

1. *Kāyānupassanā*: observation of the body
2. *Vedanānupassanā*: the observation of sensations
3. *Cittānupassanā*: the observation of mind
4. *Dhammānupassanā:* the observation of mental contents

The ultimate aim is to cleanse the mind. Nirvana is beyond mind and matter. It can come to you anytime depending on how pure you are. In that state, all your senses stop functioning. It could be for a second, a minute, or longer, but for that brief period, you are beyond all sensation, all thought. The yardstick to measure one's progress on the path is the equanimity that one has developed. Equanimity must be at the level of bodily sensations if one is to go to the depths of the mind and eradicate the impurities. If one learns to be aware of sensations and to remain equanimous towards them, it becomes easy to keep one's balance in external situations as well.

Now the question may arise in the reader's mind, "What have I gained after practicing vipasanna for so many years and attending so many courses by taking out precious time from my busy life?" The answer is rather simple. I have not attained any stage, then what I have got and why I am so regularly practicing as well as working desperately to send more and more people to attend vipasanna courses. Attending this Satipathanna course, I have been able to keep myself on the right path, working and accumulating more and more *paramis* which will result in keeping my present life and future life better. I am not worried about *anagami, sadgagami, arhant,* or Nirvana stages. I am trying to become a good human being and work for myself and others.

Uttiṭṭhe! Nappamajjeyya!

Dhammaṃ sucaritaṃ care.

Dhammacārī sukhaṃ setiṃ loke paramhi ca.

Arise! Do not be heedless!

Lead a righteous life.

The righteous live happily

both in this world and the next.

Dhammapada 13.168

REFERENCES

The Dhammapada: The Buddha's Path of Wisdom. 2008. Translated from the Pali by Acharya Buddharakkhita. Sri Lanka: Buddhist Publication Society.

Mahasatipatthana Sutta, Vipassana Research Institute (Igatpuri, India). Accessed 8/15/23, https://www.vridhamma. org/node/2786

CONTRIBUTIONS OF THE BUDDHIST PALA ERA IN THE DEVELOPMENT OF GAUDIYA DANCE AND OTHER ART FORMS OF BENGAL

Dr. Mahua Mukherjee

Retired Professor, Rabindra Bharati University

The Buddhist Pala Era made significant contributions to the development of Gaudiya dance and other art forms in Bengal. This period, which lasted for approximately 400 years from the eighth to the twelfth century CE, is often referred to as the "Golden Age" of Bengal's cultural history. The Pala rulers, who were Buddhist, played a pivotal role in promoting Buddhism and fostering the growth of various artistic, literary, religious, educational, and cultural endeavors.The Pala dynasty was established in the mid-eighth century AD, with Gopala becoming the king of Bengal after gaining the support of numerous chiefs through a bloodless revolution. The rulers of the Pala Dynasty were strong patrons of Buddhism, particularly Mahayana Buddhism, and held a position of supreme authority in the international Buddhist world. They were instrumental in spreading Buddhism to Tibet and the Southeast Asian archipelago.

Gopala was succeeded by his son Dharmapala, who reigned from approximately 770 to 810 AD. Dharmapala consolidated his power throughout North India and established an efficient government. He also played a key role in the development of education by building Buddhist universities across Bengal, including the renowned Vikramshila Mahavihara. These institutions attracted Tibetan bhikshus (monks) who came to study at Nalanda and Vikramshila, while many Acharyas (teachers) from Bengal went to Tibet to spread Buddhist teachings.

During Dharmapala's reign, Bengal experienced significant changes in political, social, and cultural spheres. The subsequent ruler, Devapala (reigned approximately 810–850 AD), further expanded his power across North India and gained fame that extended to Java, Sumatra, and the Malay Peninsula. His influence even attracted an ambassador from King Balaputradeva of the Shailendra Dynasty. Devapala served as the head of the Nalanda monastery, a renowned Buddhist academic and cultural center.

The Pala Dynasty's rule marked a peak of glory for Bengal, and it had a profound impact on the cultural history of the region. During this period, scholars like Pandit Atish Dipankar Srijnan emerged, and the individual kingdoms of Bengal patronized various cultural fields. Rampala's reign saw the composition of works such as Sandhyakara Nandi's "Ramcharita Kavya," Sridhara Bhatta's "Naisutrer Tika," and Chakrapani Dutta's "Chikitsa Sangraha." This era is also known for its academic achievements, with the establishment of Vikramshila Mahavihara and Sompura Mahavihara. Atish Dipankara Srijnan served as the Principal of

Vikramshila Mahavihara, while the ruins of Sompura Mahavihara were discovered in Paharpur. Skilled artists like Dhiman and Bitopal, as mentioned by Tibetan historian, Lama Tarnath, left their mark on this period through their exquisite artistic contributions.

Besides other mediums of art, the Pala rule deserves credit for its advancement and expansion of the art of dance. This is evident through different sculptures, literature, and paintings. In most of today's classical dances of India, Devadasis play a significant role, and Gaudiya Nritya is no exception. It has a long tradition of the Devadasi system. During the Pala period in Greater Bengal, there was a detailed practice of dance and music. Temple dancers performed in various temples during this time, as referenced in the Rajatarangini written by Kalhana, a Kashmiri poet. From this, we learn that in the eighth century in Paundravardhana, a city of today's North Bengal, Devadasis performed classical dance according to the tenets of Natyashastral.

The story goes as follows:

Once, Jayapida, the king of Kashmir (c. 751–782 AD), disguised himself and visited Paundravardhana, the capital of Gauda-Vanga in North Bengal. He witnessed a beautiful Nartaki named Kamala performing Lasya Nritya in the temple of Kartikeya, following the codification of Bharata's Natyashastra. Nartaki Kamala offered the king a betel leaf, or "Tambula," as per the existing custom of Bengal. The king was so moved and spellbound by the gesture and the gravity of the dance that he married Kamala and brought her to Kashmir. This story suggests that Kashmir had a deep appreciation for the culture of Bengal from ancient times, and it wouldn't be unwise to think that the culture of Bengal also influenced Kashmir.

We find references to devadasis as devabarabanita in the Ramacharita Kavya of Gauda poet Sandhyakara Nandi:

Paramara-vikaravir-yuvatibhir-apidevabarabanibhi kvanitvamani-kinkinikangkrita-nepathyadbhatam-natantibhi.[81]

---

81 Radhagovinda Basak, (edited & translated), *Ramacharita Kavya, Dacca*, General Printers and Publishers, 130 (Vangabda), 97.

This means that the Devabarabanitas were vigorously dancing, wearing jewelry, and fully made up. Sandhyakar Nandi's poetic work provides a reasonable description of the tempo or lasya of music, the components of makeup and costume. In verses 33–36, he mentions the names of several gems used for making jewelry during that time, such as diamond, pearl, vaiduryamani, and others. The work also mentions the types of costumes worn during that period, as well as the components of makeup, including kasturi, kalaguru, sandalwood paste, kumkum, and camphor. It also mentions the critical "laya" or tempo of the dance and music.

Apart from literature and the devadasi system, there were many renowned sculptors during the Pala period, especially during the reigns of Dharmapala and Devapala.

During their reign, Dhimana and his son Bitopala were the most famous sculptors, introducing a beautiful technique in sculpture that became known as the "Eastern Indian style." Other renowned sculptors of the Pala period include Subhota, Tatata, Vishnubhadra, and others. This Eastern Indian Style or "Purbadeshiya Reeti" helped develop sculptures and paintings in later periods in Nepal, Tibet, Assam, and other regions. The practice of painting was also deep and elaborate during this period, as evident from manuscript plates such as Patachitra.

During the Pala period, the principal substances used to make images (nritta murtis) were clay (terracotta), wood, stone, and metals. The establishment of the Buddhist Pala dynasty in Bengal around the middle of the eighth century AD marked a long period of Pala rule, spanning nearly four centuries, which witnessed the rise and growth of Buddhism not only in Bengal but also in a large part of Eastern India. This period saw the flourishing of various art forms such as stone and metal sculptures, terracotta, palm leaf paintings, and exquisite carvings on stone and other mediums. These artistic traditions not only represented the highly developed state of the arts in Bengal but also reflected ancient artistic practices. Many of the discovered images in undivided Bengal are made of black stone and generally belong to the period from 800

AD to 1280 AD.

Various centers of the image-making industry emerged in different parts of Bengal, including Amati in West Dinajpur, which was noticed among the present-day ruins of Bengal. Another significant center was observed by Bhattashali in the vicinity of Dacca[82] (now Dhaka). The finest examples of Pala craftsmanship can be seen in numerous metal images found in Greater Bengal. Ancient discoveries inform us that Chandraketugarh in West Bengal was also an important site for metal crafts during the early historic period in Eastern India.[83]

Bengal, known for its abundance of Greenwood trees, possesses a rich tradition of wooden images. The wooden carvers of Bengal, belonging to the artisan community called Sutradhara, have contributed significantly to the history of wood carving in Eastern India.[84]

Terracotta sculptures, also known as clay images, hold great importance in the artistic techniques of Bengal. The clay soil prevalent in Bengal, especially along the Ganga and Brahmaputra rivers, facilitated the flourishing of this art form in the riverine plains of Bengal since ancient times. Significant collections of terracotta sculptures have been unearthed during excavations at Paharpur (present-day Bangladesh) and Jagjibanpur (present-day West Bengal) dating back to the ninth century AD, during the Pala period.

The Buddhist Palas developed a distinct local expression, evolving their own characteristics, which persisted for about 400 years until the arrival of the Muslims. Bengal is rightfully considered a museum of architecture.

---

82 P.K. Bhattacharya, *Iconography of Sculptures, North Bengal, Akshay Kmar Maitreya Museum*, University of North Bengal,   1983, pg. introduction.
83 Chattopadhyay, Pranab, Kr., Metal finds from Chandraketugarh, *Kolkata Archaeology of Eastern India*, Centre of Archaeological Studies and Training, Eastern India, 2002, 454.
84 Chakraborti, Shyamal, *Wood Carvings of Bengal in Gurusaday Dutta Museum*, Kolkata, Gurusaday Dutta Museum, 2001, 7–9.

REFERENCES

- Bhattacharya, P.K., *Iconography of Sculptures, North Bengal, Akshay Kmar Maitreya Museum,* University of North Bengal, 1983.

- Chakraborti, Shyamal, *Wood Carvings of Bengal in Gurusaday Dutta Museum*, Kolkata, Gurusaday Dutta Museum, 2001.

- Chattopadhyay, Pranab, Kr., *Metal Finds from Chandraketugarh,* Kolkata Archaeology of Eastern India, Centre of Archaeological Studies and Training, Eastern India, 2002.

- Radhagovinda Basak, (edited & translated), *Ramacharita Kavya, Dacca*, General Printers and Publishers, 130 (Vangabda).

BUDDHISM AND TAGORE'S CHANDALIKA

Dr. Satabdi Acharyya

Independent Scholar and Icon of Goudiya Dance, Kolkata

Ancient Bengal was a major center of Buddhist learning, art, and imperialism; indeed, Buddhism is the basis of Bengal's cultural and linguistic heritage-the earliest poem-song in Bengali is "Charyapada," which was composed by the Buddhist *sahajiya siddhacharyas* or monk-gurus. According to contemporary scholars, the term Dharma in Bengali means "Bauddha Dharma" (Buddhadharma) or Buddhism and the term dharmapuja means "Buddhapuja" or worship of Buddha. When Buddhism began to decline in different parts of India, it took its last shelter in Bengal.

From time immemorial, travelers and pilgrims have longed to explore Bengal's magnificent monasteries, stupas, chaityas (prayer halls), and ancient seats of learning. Through the ages, such travelers have been a valuable source of information and recorded evidence in their travelogues. If we study only the archeological evidence of Buddhism's past, we may arrive at mistaken conclusions because unless Buddhist texts, literature, paintings, sculpture are also studied comparatively, the soul of Buddhism or the Buddha's wisdom cannot be properly understood.

Tagore was influenced by the Upaniṣads, Buddhism and other scriptures. He developed his concept of philosophy from Upaniṣad, Buddhism, Bāuls, folk singers and others mystic saints like Lalan, Kabir. Examples of Tagore's devotion to Buddhist culture is found through his various works. Tagore as a metaphysical poet was influenced by Indian Scriptures such as the Upaniṣads and Vedānta. He frequently and spontaneously recited Buddhist hymns. This influence lasted long, till his death. It was not because he was born in a Hindu family but because the philosophy of those scriptures shaped his own way of life and helped him reach the highest goal of human aspiration. Tagore's emphasis on the all-pervasive character of God, his assertion of the kinship between "man and man" and between "man and nature" are all taken from the Upaniṣads. He was also fully acquainted with the entire Upaniṣadic tradition and as such carried the stamp of some of the Vedāntic system in his thought. Vaiṣṇavism, a sect of Vedānta, made him realize the necessity and importance of opening the ways of the heart for apprehending the one.

Rabindranath brought harmony between the Finite and the Infinite. To him such harmony remains within a man. An individual's ego wants to bind him to this worldly object while his soul longs for the Infinite. Freedom, for Tagore, is a freedom from bondage created by alienation. Buddhism also shaped Tagore's own metaphysical philosophy as the verses of Upaniṣads. Tagore said, "To me the verses of the Upanishads and the teachings of the Buddha have ever been thing of the spirit, and therefore endowed with boundless vital growth as being instinct with individual meaning for me, as for others, and awaiting for their confirmation my own special testimony, which must have its value because of its individuality." (Sadhana– The Realisation of Life by Rabindranath Tagore). It is clear to us from his own words how he was influenced by Buddha. Tagore was impressed by Bāul singers of Bengal, Kabir, and other mystic saints. The unsophisticated theology and the simple ways of the Bāuls impressed Tagore very much. Besides the Bāuls, the mystic saints like Kabir and others always held a special fascination for Tagore. Under these influences Tagore shaped his own religion, the Religion of Man and composed many poems, songs, novels, and paintings for us.

In his critical appreciation of the Dhammapada Tagore says, "Materials of different shades of Indian thought and culture are confined in Buddhist literature and due to the lack of intimacy with them the entire history of India remains unfulfilled. Being convinced of it, cannot a few youths of our country dedicate themselves for the restoration of the Buddhist heritage and make it a mission in life?" Rabindranath Tagore & Buddhist Culture, Sudhanshu Bimal Barua, 1961, Buddhist Publication Society Kandy, Sri Lanka.

At that time Tagore introduced Buddhism as a special course of study for the students of Santiniketan. To widen the knowledge of Buddhism he deputed Professor Nitai Benode Goswami to go to Ceylon, the bastion of Buddhism. The center of Buddhist studies augmented by Tagore at Santiniketan is today one of the greatest symposiums of Buddhist culture.

Tagore, popular for his dance dramas and ballads, found the source of his prose drama *Chandalika* from "Shardula Karnabadaan" extracted from Nepali Buddhist literature, edited by Rajendralal Mitra. Tagore staged many performances of Chandalika at Shantiniketan. In 1935, Pratima Debi started with the rehearsals, and it was staged on the sixteenth of March with Nandalal Basu's daughter as the protagonist. In 1939, *Chandalika* was staged again for the ruler of Tripura. Tagore choose the characters himself:

Prakriti – Nandita

Mother – Mrinalini Sarabhai

Buddhist monk Ananda – Kelu

Nair Curd seller – Anangalal

Bangle seller – Maki

Village damsels – Sukriti, Anu, Mamata, and others

One look at the list of dancers makes us understand the fusion of different dance styles in performance-Kandi, Bharatnatyam, Kathakali and dances from Japan and Europe. It was staged again in 1940 for Mahatma Gandhi.

Each ballad by Tagore is based on some basic human value, more precious than religion in the ordinary sense. Love, compassion, mercy, sympathy, kindness, a sense of just and unjust attitude, a sense of morality from the core of the human heart are those human values.

Self-consciousness, up to a point, is necessary for self-development; for without an awareness of the dignity of one's own role or function, one cannot give one's best to the world.

The above are the lines from Rabindranath Tagore's *Chandalika*, a drama with a lot of love, compassion, feelings of inferiority, new birth, and culmination of the great teachings of Buddha. This drama has a vast history and has been portrayed over centuries as a musical drama. The music gives more life to the play, and makes the audience understand the intensity of the emotions that the protagonists carry in themselves during the play.

The venue of the story is Sravasti, the famous ancient Indian city. Lord Buddha was residing in the garden house of his disciple Anāthapindādā. Ānanda, another disciple, the hero of the drama, while returning to the monastery after taking his midday meal with a family of his inmate, felt thirsty. He saw Prakriti, a Chandal girl, fetching water from a well. Ānanda wanted water from her. After some hesitation, she served him water to quench his thirst. Ānanda blessed her and went away. Just after this event Prakriti become tremendously attracted to Ānanda. But finding no easy way to win this celebrated monk, she resorted to her mother, well-versed in black magic and sorcery. Prakriti's mother raised an altar of cow dung in the courtyard, lit a fire and performed her black magic by offering 108 arka flowers in the fire. Being unable to resist the charm Ānanda became extremely repentant, began to cry and mentally surrendered to the Lord Buddha. Buddha could understand the situation by virtue of his omniscience. He recited appropriate chants. The spell of the black magic subsided. Ānanda came back to the monastery. Tagore moderated this original story a bit to suit his drama and dance-drama. In Tagore's creativity we find that both Prakriti and her mother became repentant for bringing down the divine monk Ānanda to worldly sensuality. They prayed for his forgiveness, bowed down to him, and Ānanda blessed them along with chanting, "Buddho śuddho karuṇāmahannabo."

Buddha is the ocean of compassion and bliss. This drama shows that love knows no bounds, no one can be of lower birth, real bliss wins over erotic sensuality and evil spells of life are but passing phases of our journey towards a tranquil and enlightened state. Tagore glorified the eternal virtues of Buddhism through the *Malini*, *Chandalika*, and *Natir Puja*, three dramas based on Buddhist stories. In the *Malini*, universal Buddhist tolerance is established against narrow sectarianism of the Brahmanical religion. In the *Chandalika*, the revolutionary spirit of Tagore is manifested through the character of Prakriti, a Chandala girl, low-born and untouchable. She bursts out, "Many Chandalas abound in the country in the houses of Brahmins; I cannot be a Chandala."

A religion that insults is a false religion. Everyone united to make me conform to a creed that blinds and gags. But since that day something forbids me to conform any longer. I'm afraid of nothing now.

The story that is revealed in the plot is all about discovering new dimensions of life, as well as discovering one's inner self. The story has to offer many aspects of human approaches, such as obsession with something can be as disastrous as gulping poison. Another aspect of the play is covered through the act of quenching the thirst of a Buddhist monk. That proves to be a kind of "rebirth" for a girl who is meant to be untouchable. The presence of the mother is a cue saying that one should not step out of the boundaries that are set by religion and society for any person living on this earth. Rebellion against the wall of system and society is another thing portrayed by the drama. The presence of a Buddhist monk in the play rejuvenates it, bringing a whole new sense to the play and the teachings of Buddha, determination towards life, and bringing up the best in a person are the things that convert it into a multi-dimensional and psychological drama of intense spiritual conflict. Finally, turning into a sort of redemption, along with self-realization, the drama yet has a tale to tell, that *love does not claim possession, but it gives freedom.*

It is, Ananda, the monk, pure as heaven, beautiful, enlightened, who has renounced the earthly pleasures, who approaches her to quench his thirst. But, being a Chandal, Prakriti was bound not to offer him water from a lake as impure as herself, on which he laments, and speaks to her, "If the black clouds of *sravana* are dubbed Chandel, what of it? It doesn't change their nature or destroy the virtue of their water. Don't humiliate yourself; self-humiliation is a sin, worse than self-murder.

It is when comes the twist in the tale, when she revealed a new birth of herself and is determined to bring him back to her, that she discovers and cherishes her new birth with herself. No doubt, the Hindu concept of caste distinction based on one's birth is inhuman. It should be completely wiped out and equality tinged with humanity should be established. This is the order of the day. Yet, for the better functioning of the social order, some moral and ethical restraints should also be exercised by the newly awakened human beings. This could be the idea of Tagore in dramatizing the Ananda legend through *Chandalika*. In the words of K.R. Kripalani, "New consciousness after ages of suppression is overpowering and one learns restraint only after suffering," (Kulkarni, 2014). That's what happens to the protagonist of *Chandalika*. Prakriti, the Chandal girl, in the end of her tragic experience, realizes the necessity of ethical values in her new birth. The enlightened mind of Prakriti now refuses to accept the age-old humiliating cannons of Hindu religion. For her, "A religion that insults is a false religion. Everyone united to make me conform to a creed that blinds and gags" (Kulkarni, 2014). Ananda's preaching, brings a sea change in her attitude and she feels awakened to a new life-a life where she is no Chandal but a human being at par with the world, even with the holy man. She argues with her mother: "Plenty of slaves are born of royal blood, but I am no slave; plenty of Chandals are born of Brahmin families, but I am no Chandal" (Kulkarni, 2014, p 152).

Dr. Ambedkar, the modern social reformer and messiah of the downtrodden, is once said to have remarked, "Make aware the slave of his slavery, and he would revolt" (Ambedkar, 2023). Similar things happen with the untouchable Prakriti. The "free mind" now fires the emotions of love and desire for Ananda in her heart. Excited by the feelings of liberty and to prove her equal status, she revolts against the age-old shackles of the marginality put upon her "self" by the religion and society. She now decides to get united with the very person who had liberated this "self." This is an outrageous idea for the moral and ethical cannons of the world since the Buddhist monks in their pursuit of Nirvana follow the vow of celibacy strictly and so are beyond the reach of any common individual in terms of worldly pleasures and familial obligations. Prakriti loses all sense of fear for the holiness and social and religious codes of conduct in her newly awakened state. Hence, she declares: "I fear nothing any longer, except to sink back again, to forget myself again, to enter again the house of darkness. That would be worse than death!" (Ambedkar, 2023, p. 153). In doing so, she forgets that Ananda is not an ordinary human being to exercise her passions upon, but a divine mortal working for the cause of upliftment of human dignity. She says to her mother: "I'll send my call into his soul, for him to hear. I am longing to give myself; it is like a pain at my heart" (Ambedkar, 2023, p. 152). This pain of longing for the beautiful and magnificent monk becomes even more intense when, later in the play during her second chance citing him, Ananda, immersed in his inner spiritual self, totally ignores her presence, and moves on chanting the hymn of Lord Buddha. That crashes her illusionary flight of worldly longing. It is a great shock to her sensitive mind. Her female ego gets crushed and the newly awakened woman feels deeply hurt. In rage, she orders her mother to cast her magical spell on the male heart of Ananda to force him to beg for her conjugal company. Prakriti's mother works her magical spell upon the meditating Ananda who is resting at his abode in his spiritual bliss. He is helpless as he trudges all the way from his monsoon meditation abode at Vaisali to Prakriti's residence in Sravasti. That is a victory of Prakriti's marginalized womanhood against the rigid spiritual morals of the monk.

But this victory of the marginalized girl, however, remains short-lived. When Ananda is at the threshold of her home, she is horrified at the change in him brought about by her mother's magic. The light, radiance, and the shining purity has vanished from the beautiful and serene face of Ananda due to the mother's spell. He appears to her completely worn out, faded and without heavenly glow. He does not even look like the revered monk whom she earnestly wanted to wed. His ugly face strikes Prakriti beyond her belief. In shock, she realizes her mistake and the sin she had committed in her blind rage.

Repenting, she stops her mother from further exercising the spell, begs forgiveness from Ananda and falls at his feet. As a consequence, the magical spell, which so far tormented the pure heart of the monk, breaks to normalcy. The mother, too, begging forgiveness, dies at the feet of the holy man. And Ananda returns, chanting the name of the purest Buddha, to his usual self with untainted spirituality. Prakriti, the Chandal girl, at the end of her tragic experience, realizes the necessity of ethical values in her new birth. Eventually, she corrects the mistake of overhauling the human ethics she had committed earlier and turns a better and spiritual woman in the end.

REFERENCES

- Ambedkar, B.R. 2023. *The Untouchables*. New Delhi: Namaskar Books.

- Barua, Sudhanshu Bimal. 1978. "Rabindranath Tagore and Buddhist Culture." Sri Lanka: Buddhist Publication

Society.

- Houseal, Joseph. 2020. "Three Aspects of Buddhist Dance." Buddhist Door Global website. https://www.buddhistdoor.net/features/three-aspects-of-buddhist-dance/

- Kulkarni, P.D. 2014. "Chandalika," *The Criterion: An International Journal in English.*

- Mohammad, Shafiullah S. 2019. "A Study of Rabindranath Tagore's Chandalika as a Psychological Play of Intense Spiritual Conflict." *Global Academic Journal of Linguistics and Literature,* 2019, 1(1) 20–21. https://gajrc.com/journal/gajll/home

- Mukherjee, Mahua, 2008. "Bharatiya Nritya Troi." Kolkata: Sanskrit Sahitya Parishad.

SERENITY ANDAWAKENING: BUDDHIST INFLUENCES IN RABINDRANATH TAGORE'S POETRY

Monikiran Dattagupta

PhD Research Scholar

Lovely Professional University, Punjab

Abstract

*T*his paper explores the profound Buddhist influences evident in Rabindranath Tagore's poetry, focusing on four of his notable works: "Abhisar," "Mulyaprapti," "Nagarlokkhi," and "Pujarini." Through a close analysis of these poems, the paper illuminates Tagore's engagement with Buddhist philosophy and its impact on his poetic expression. Themes of compassion, interconnectedness, and the pursuit of inner peace are examined, revealing Tagore's deep understanding of the transformative power of mindfulness and empathy. By delving into the complexities of existence and the interconnected nature of all beings, Tagore's works serve as a timeless reminder of the profound teachings of Buddhism and invite readers on a journey of self-discovery and contemplation.

Introduction

Rabindranath Tagore (1861–1941), the celebrated poet, writer, and philosopher, was profoundly influenced by Buddhism, and this influence shines through in his literary works. Tagore's writing reflects the timeless wisdom and spiritual depth of Buddhist philosophy as he explores themes of compassion, interconnectedness, and the pursuit of inner peace. Through his works, Tagore invites readers on a journey of self-discovery and contemplation, delving into the complexities of existence and the interconnected nature of all beings. His writings serve as a gentle reminder of the transformative power of mindfulness and empathy, offering readers a profound glimpse into the profound teachings of Buddhism. Four of his creations have been chosen for in-depth study of this subject. They are "Abhisar," "Mulyaprapti," "Nagarlokkhi," and "Pujarini."

1. Abhisar

Summary: During a monsoon evening, Upagupta, a monk, found himself resting on a street when suddenly a young maiden named Basabdatta accidentally trampled upon him. In her haste to meet her lover, she immediately apologized to the monk and invited him to her house as a gesture of repentance. However, the monk politely declined, stating that it was not the appropriate time for him to visit her home. He assured her that when the right time arrived, he would surely pay her a visit.

Several months later, on a late spring evening, Upagupta came across a woman suffering from smallpox who had been cast out of the city due to the contagious nature of her illness. To his astonishment, he realized that it was Basabdatta herself who lay abandoned and neglected. Without hesitation, the monk rushed to her side, disregarding the fears surrounding the disease. He gently cradled her head in his lap, an act considered exceptionally noble, as individuals with smallpox were often avoided and considered untouchable. During that time, smallpox had become an epidemic, causing villages to turn into necropolises.

Upagupta began chanting holy prayers, invoking divine blessings for her healing, and applied soothing sandalwood to alleviate her suffering. Basabdatta was deeply moved by the monk's compassion and fearlessness. Despite the entire city shunning her and excluding her from their boundaries, Upagupta, without any fear of contagion, tended to her with unwavering devotion and care. He explained that it was at that moment, when she was in dire need and society had rejected her, that the correct time had finally arrived for him to fulfil his promise and offer his assistance.

Analysis: Upagupta, a Buddhist monk, exemplified the teachings of Buddha through his remarkable control over his temper and his renouncement of material desires. When Basabdutta accidentally trampled on him, Upagupta responded with utmost politeness, showcasing the virtue of tolerance preached by Buddha. Despite Basabdutta's offer of shelter, Upagupta declined, adhering to his vow of renunciation.

Basabdutta, filled with remorse, realized her unintentional act and offered Upagupta a warm and cozy shelter. Her compassion and concern for his well-being demonstrated her understanding of Buddhist principles. However, the city guards heartlessly expelled Basabdutta during the spring festivities, leaving her afflicted with pox and without any support.

In her desperate condition, Basabdutta encountered Upagupta, who fearlessly approached her despite the contagious disease. His selfless actions of applying soothing sandal paste and praying for her recovery exemplified compassion and selflessness. Upagupta's dedication to caring for Basabdutta without expecting personal gain reflected the virtues taught by Buddha.

This poem contrasts the characters' actions to highlight the essence of Buddhism. Upagupta's control over his temper, renunciation of desires, and care for others exemplify Buddhist principles. In contrast, Basabdutta's mistreatment and abandonment expose the absence of compassion. Upagupta's actions demonstrate the transformative power of Buddhism and its potential impact on individuals and society.

2. Mulyaprapti

Summary: During the late autumn season, when the final lotus of the year bloomed, Sudas, a humble gardener, carefully plucked it and hurried towards the palace with the intention of selling it at a higher value. His heart was set on approaching the king and requesting an audience. Along the way, a passer-by noticed the exquisite flower and inquired about its price. He wished to offer it to Lord Buddha, who happened to be visiting the city that day. Sudas proposed a price of one unit of gold for the rare lotus, and the passer-by agreed to purchase it at that amount.

Suddenly, the king entered the court and caught sight of the captivating lotus. Curious about its value, he inquired about its price, as he too planned to present it to Lord Buddha during his visit. Sudas informed the king that the stranger had already agreed to pay one unit of gold. Hearing this, the king promptly raised the price to ten units of gold for the same flower. The stranger swiftly matched the bid and declared that he would buy it for twenty units of gold. The bidding war escalated between the two, with the price of the lotus soaring rapidly.

As a poor gardener, Sudas was astonished by the exorbitant sums being offered for a seemingly ordinary lotus. He pondered that if both the stranger and the king were willing to pay such immense amounts, then the one they sought to offer the lotus to, Lord Buddha, must hold it in even higher regard and would be willing to pay an even greater price. Filled with this realization, Sudas made a decision. He refused to sell the lotus and rushed to visit Buddha.

Upon finally meeting Buddha, Sudas found himself overwhelmed by the presence and aura of the enlightened one. In that moment, his desire for profit and material gain vanished. Astonished by Buddha's divine personality, Sudas humbly offered the lotus at his feet. When Buddha asked Sudas what he prayed for, the gardener replied with utmost humility that he desired nothing more than a tiny particle of dust from Buddha's sacred feet.

Analysis: Sudas, an impoverished gardener, initially approaches the king driven by his desire to maximize profit from the last lotus of the season. Engaging in a bidding process with a stranger and the king, Sudas realizes they are competing for the lotus in the assumption that Buddha would greatly value it. This realization leads to a profound transformation within Sudas. He understands that something more meaningful than financial gain is at stake.

Upon meeting Buddha, Sudas undergoes a deeper transformation. He realizes that money alone cannot provide true fulfillment or lasting happiness. In the presence of Buddha's enlightenment, Sudas experiences a spiritual awakening and gains a deeper understanding of life's meaning. Overwhelmed by this newfound perception, Sudas humbly offers the lotus at Buddha's feet, seeking spiritual blessings.

Sudas represents the archetype of an economic man initially motivated solely by profit. However, his encounter with Buddha leads to a shift in perspective. He recognizes the higher values and blessings that cannot be measured in monetary terms. Sudas's journey reflects the teachings of Buddhism, highlighting the importance of spiritual growth, self-realization, and the understanding that true happiness transcends the pursuit of wealth and material possessions.

3. Nagarlokkhi

Summary: In the drought-stricken city of Srabastipur, where poverty was rampant and people struggled to sustain themselves, Buddha recognized the dire situation and called upon his disciples to take responsibility for the welfare of the needy. However, Ratnakar Seth, a wealthy businessman, declined to undertake this task, citing his reluctance. Jayasen, an army general, expressed his willingness to sacrifice his own blood if it could help, but confessed his financial limitations in alleviating the city's poverty. Dharmapala, a prosperous farmer, lamented the infertility of his land, unable even to pay the royal tax.

As the other devotees remained silent, Buddha found himself at a loss, unable to devise a solution to feed the impoverished. It was then that Supriya, a bhikkhuni and daughter of a Buddhist monk, humbly stepped forward and offered herself to undertake the responsibility of feeding the poor. Buddha was astonished by her decision and questioned how she, as a bhikkhuni who relied on alms for her own sustenance, possessed the courage to take on such a monumental duty of providing for an entire city when wealthier individuals had refused.

With utmost humility, Supriya responded that her begging bowl was all she possessed, along with the sympathy and support of all those who would help fill it with alms. She pledged to utilize these offerings to feed every person in need. Her selfless determination moved Buddha, and he acknowledged her noble resolve to assist the suffering citizens of Srabastipur.

Analysis: In Srabastipur, Buddha faced a dilemma when wealthy individuals declined, and others had financial limitations in caring for the city's impoverished residents. However, Supriya, a bhikkhuni with only her begging bowl and the support of others, stepped forward humbly to undertake the responsibility. Her selfless determination exemplified Buddhist principles of compassion and selflessness, despite her own meager means. Buddha was deeply moved and recognized the nobility in her decision. Inspired by Supriya's example, the people of Srabastipur joined forces, contributing to the alleviation of poverty, and fostering unity and empathy. This poem highlights the contrast between the reluctance of the wealthy and Supriya's selflessness, emphasizing the transformative power of individual acts of kindness. Supriya's actions serve as a reminder of the importance of addressing the needs of the vulnerable and the profound impact that selfless actions can have on individuals and communities, embodying the core teachings of Buddhism.

4. Pujarini

Summary: Bimbisar, a king and devoted follower of Buddha,

constructed an enormous stupa using a chip of fingernail obtained from Buddha himself. Every evening, all the women of the royal family would gather to offer prayers at this stupa. However, when Ajatasatru ascended to the throne after his father, he imposed a ban on Buddhism and ordered the burning of all Buddhist scriptures during a Hindu ritual. He proclaimed that the Vedas, the Brahmins, and the king were supreme, and nothing else should be worshipped within the kingdom.

On that particular evening, Srimati, a maid who was also a fervent devotee of Buddha, approached Ajatasatru's mother with a tray adorned with flowers and a lamp, intending to make an offering to Lord Buddha as she did every day. The queen mother refused to accompany her, fearing that it would be considered disobedience to the king's decree. Undeterred, Srimati then approached the queen, Amita, and the princess, Shukla, but both were too afraid to go against the king's orders and join in the worship ritual.

Srimati wandered through the city, calling out to everyone, urging them to join her in prayer, just like every other day. However, people either fled from her in fear or drove her away, terrified of the king's wrath. As the sun set and the time for worship approached, the king's guards noticed the stupa adorned with prayer lamps. They swiftly confronted Srimati, accusing her of treason. When asked who she was, she proudly declared herself a slave of Buddha. The guards mercilessly killed her on the spot, and her blood stained the white stone of the stupa. From that day onwards, no prayer lamp was ever lit at the stupa again.

Analysis: This poem contrasts the devotion and bravery of Srimati, a maid and follower of Buddha, with the oppressive actions of King Ajatasatru, who banned Buddhism. Despite the ban, Srimati persisted in her daily prayers at the stupa, even as others hesitated due to fear of the king. She called on the city's inhabitants to join her but was met with rejection and fear. When guards accused her of treason, Srimati proudly declared herself a slave of Buddha and was killed on the spot, staining the stupa's white stone with her blood. This act resulted in the cessation of prayer lamp offerings at the stupa.

This poem underscores the themes of devotion, courage, and persecution in Buddhism. Srimati's unwavering dedication to her beliefs and her call for collective worship demonstrate the essence of Buddhist teachings. The tragic sacrifice she made highlights the challenges and sacrifices faced by those who uphold their spiritual convictions despite oppression. It serves as a reminder of the immense strength and unwavering faith that can be found within individuals committed to their spiritual path, even in the face of grave adversity.

Discussion: Rabindranath Tagore's works, although not explicitly rooted in Buddhism, often convey universal spiritual themes that resonate with Buddhist principles. Tagore himself was deeply influenced by various philosophical and spiritual traditions, including Hinduism, Vaishnavism, and the Upanishads, which shaped his worldview and artistic expressions. As he writes:

Where the mind is led forward by thee,
Into ever-widening thought and action,
Into that heaven of freedom, my Father, let my country awake.

He does not restrict humanity in the frame of any particular religion but believes in universal brotherhood. While his writings reflect a broad range of ideas, there are several aspects that showcase an affinity with Buddhism.

Transcendence of the self: Tagore's poetry frequently explores the concept of self-transcendence, moving beyond the limitations of the ego and embracing a wider, interconnected consciousness. This idea resonates with the Buddhist concept of *anatta*, which emphasizes the absence of a permanent, independent self. Tagore's poems often invite readers to move beyond the narrow boundaries of individuality and connect with the larger human experience.

Interconnectedness and unity: Buddhism teaches the

interconnectedness of all beings, and Tagore's works often reflect a similar understanding. His poetry celebrates the unity of humanity, nature, and the divine. Tagore's vision emphasizes the harmony between individuals and the world, urging a sense of oneness and compassion for all living beings. For example, Supriya had the guts to gain humility from the whole society unified, to help her feed the poor, she believed no one would turn her down if she begged for alms.

Impermanence and change: Buddhist philosophy places great emphasis on the impermanence of all things.

Similarly, Tagore's poetry frequently explores the transient nature of life, the passing of seasons, and the constant flux of emotions. For example, in "Mulyaprapti," there is a complete change in Sudas's thought process when he comes to Buddha with the flower. His writings often evoke a sense of impermanence, reminding readers of the importance of embracing change and living fully in the present moment.

Quest for enlightenment: While Tagore's focus was not explicitly on attaining enlightenment, many of his works reveal a deep longing for spiritual awakening and a search for higher truths. This resonates with the core aspiration of Buddhism, which seeks to attain enlightenment and liberation from suffering. Tagore's writings often evoke a sense of spiritual yearning and a quest for deeper meaning in life. In Abhisar, Basabdutta was enlightened when she was rescued by the monk when no other soul tended to her and left her out to die. In Mulyaprapti, Sudas was also enlightened when he saw Buddha.

Conclusion

It's important to note that Tagore's engagement with spirituality was not confined to any specific tradition, including Buddhism. His works exhibit a broad, inclusive approach that draws inspiration from various sources, enabling readers to find resonance with different philosophical and spiritual paths. Tagore's literary contributions continue to inspire individuals across cultures and religions, emphasizing themes of interconnectedness, love, and the pursuit of truth, which can be appreciated by those with an interest in Buddhism and other spiritual traditions.

Acknowledgements

I am deeply grateful to Dr. Mahua Mukherjee and my mother, Madhumita Dattagupta, for their unwavering support and guidance throughout my academic journey. Their expertise and encouragement have enhanced my understanding of the subject matter. Dr. Mukherjee's mentorship and my mother's guidance have been invaluable. They have made immense contributions in helping me understand and analyze the subject matter in the truest sense. My father, Asim Dattagupta, has inspired me all along throughout this study. I would like to extend my gratitude to Mahathero Buddhapriya for this opportunity.

REFERENCES

- Tagore, R. Kotha. *Rabindrarachanabali* (Birth Centenary edition). Kolkata: Sri Saraswati Press Ltd., 1961, 626, 638, 640, 623.

ASHOKA AND BUDDHISM

Shruti Barua

A Devotee, Sodpur, Kolkata

$\mathcal{K}$ing Asoka was one of 101 sons of King Bindusara who had sixteen wives. His name means "No Sorrow." His eldest brother, Prince Susima, plotted to kill Asoka's wife and child but his mother intervened and was killed instead. Because of this event, Prince Asoka was driven by hatred and vengeance-he killed all his brothers except one brother. He began conquest of neighboring territories with furious wars.

After the Kalinga war, the brutality of the conquest and the sight of the aftermath led Asoka to adopt Buddhism. He used his position to propagate the relatively new religion to new heights, as far as ancient Rome and Egypt. He made Buddhism his state religion around 260 BC, and propagated and preached it within his domain and worldwide from about 250 BC. Asoka undoubtedly has to be credited with the first serious attempt to develop a Buddhist policy.

1. Dhamma Vijaya

After the Kalinga war and his conversion to Buddhism, Asoka ceased *digvijaya* or "conquest by war" and embarked on *dhammavijaya*, meaning "conquest by Dhamma." His reign became more humane as he ruled according to the Dhamma. He was the first king to build major edicts with Buddhist inscriptions all over India and Central Asia. He set up a department of religious officers to look into moral education for the people. He went on *dhammayatra* (pilgrimages) to the holy places. He was generous with the requisites for the Sangha and supported them handsomely. His son and daughter joined the Sangha, spreading the Dhamma most successfully in Sri Lanka. He claimed to his nighbors that he had no expansionist intentions towards countries bordering his empire.

After the Third Buddhist Council, missionary work to the adjacent nine countries saw the spread of Theravada Buddhism under his patronage. The nine countries are: Kashmir and Gandhara (N. Punjab), Mahisamandala (south of Vindhyan mountains), Vanavasi (N. Kanara), Aparantaka (N. Gujarat, Kathiawar, Kacch, and Sind), Maharattha (country of the Marathi, modern Bombay), Yona countries (clans of foreign race on NW frontier, Greeco-Bactrian Kingdom), Himavanta (Himalayan region), Suvannabhumi (Lower Myanmar, Thailand, Java and even Malaya) and Tambapanni (Sri Lanka).

The most important and successful mission was to Sri Lanka. It was led by King Asoka's own son, Venerable Mahinda, who converted the Sri Lankan king, and eventually all his subjects to Buddhism. The Tipitaka was also brought over and eventually compiled into writing in Sri Lanka about 300 years later.

2. Firm and Humane Rule

Asoka's rule became more humane and went according to the Dhamma. He told his people that he considered them as his own children with nothing to fear from him. He promised ready access to them and their problems. He pursued an official policy of nonviolence (*ahimsa*). Animal sacrifices were prohibited. Cruelty to domestic and wild animals was prohibited. Hunting certain wild animals was banned. Only limited hunting was permitted for consumption reasons. King Asoka promoted the concept of vegetarianism.

Forest and wildlife reserves were established; the burning of forests was prohibited. Hospitals for people and animals were built. Medical herbs were cultivated. He had wells dug, trees planted, and rest houses built. He took care of the old, ascetics, widowed, and prisoners. Spurning handlooms were provided for widows as a form of employment.

He encouraged fasting and meritorious deeds to be done by prisoners. He urged criminals to see the blunders of their crimes. Citizens were fined for littering or if they did not help in putting out fires.

3. Department of Religious Officers

Asoka created this ministry in the thirteenth year after his rule. It was staffed by high officials to focus on the following:

Moral education for the people

Various of performances of gods

Improvement of jail administration (as inscribed on Rock Edict V)

Humanization of ruthless criminal laws (Pillar Edict IV)

Enforcement of various regulations of piety (Pillar Edict V and VI)

These projects were carried out throughout his empire. To ensure that they were done, Asoka went on frequent inspection tours. The protection and promotion of all religions, and the fostering of inter-religious harmony was seen as one of the duties of the state.

The Department of Religious Affairs of Dhammamatras was established to look after the affairs of various religious bodies and to encourage the practice of religion. Ashoka offered generously to all religious practitioners. In the twelfth year of his reign, he bestowed an excavated dwelling and shrines to the Ajivika community.

4. Pilgrimage

In the past, kings would go out on journeys (*yatra*) for pleasure, such as hunting expeditions and other similar enjoyments. But King Asoka went out on pilgrimages (*dhammayatra*) to the holy places. He would donate to religious practitioners and assist elders with money, instruct and discuss Dhamma with the citizens.

He visited Bodh Gaya in the tenth year of his rule. Pillars and edicts were established in the Buddhist sacred places to mark his visit. The Lumbini Edict was erected when he visited the birthplace of the Buddha in the twentieth year of his reign. To commemorate his visit, he exempted the local people from paying taxes to his government.

5. Dharma Conquest of Neighboring Land

The kingdoms surrounding his, so easily conquered, were instead made to be well-respected allies. Without any war or any aggressive policy, he maintained a large empire and had friendly relations with foreign powers.

Instead of organizing military expedition against other countries, he was busy organizing peace missions under his *duta* for the purpose of humanitarian work (building hospitals, supplying medicinal herbs, building wells, and sending engineers to assist when needed) in those foreign countries. Silenced was the war drum (*bheri-ghosa*), replaced by *dhammaghosa*. Asoka stands out as the pioneer of peace and universal brotherhood in history.

According to many European and Asian historians, the age of Asoka was the age of light and delight. He was perhaps the first emperor in human history who taught the lesson of unity, peace, equality, and love within and outside his empire.

In Asoka's own words, the Dhamma *vijaya*, a moral conquest, was the principal conquest. The only true conquest lies in the conquest of self by Dhamma. A king should first subdue himself and then seek to subdue his foes. How could a king who has not been able to conquer his own self be able to conquer his foes.

6. Construction of Religious Monuments

Ashoka used much of his wealth for religious education and building monasteries and monuments. He built the great stupa of Sanchi and erected several thousand Buddhist monuments to enshrine the Buddha's relics. He built viharas for the monks and the famous vihara in Pataliputra was named after him. Ashoka also helped to develop viharas (intellectual hubs) such as Nalanda and Taxila and many temples, including Sanchi and Mahabodhi.

7. Buddhist Edicts and Monuments

Ashoka's pronouncements were written on rocks on the periphery of his kingdom, while pillars were erected along the main roads and where pilgrims gathered. His edicts were written in his own words and these edicts were found in more than thirty places throughout India, Nepal, Pakistan, and Afghanistan. Most of them were written in the native language of the place.

Asoka was engaged in spreading Buddhism through the rock, stone, and pillar edicts erected in his empire and beyond. The Bhabru inscription called upon his people to respect and have faith in Buddha, Dhamma, and Sangha.

The individual morality that Asoka hoped to foster included respect towards parents, elders, teachers, friends, servants, ascetics, and brahmins. Girnar Rock Edict Three stressed filial duties.

He also encouraged generosity (*dana*), harmlessness towards life (*avihimsa bhutanam*), moderation in spending and saving, and treating others properly. The qualities of heart that were recommended by Asoka in the edicts indicate his deep spirituality. They include kindness, self-examination, truthfulness, gratitude and purity of heart, enthusiasm, loyalty, self-control, and love of Dhamma.

The following seven Buddhist texts were encouraged for both Sangha and lay disciples. These texts favored by Asoka appeared to bear on the life of the monks and the ethical standards to which Asoka was devoted. Asoka did not concern himself with the philosophy of Buddhism, but in the ethical and practical application.

The texts are Vinayasamukkase, Ariyavasani, Anagata Bhayani, Muni Gatha, Mauneya Sutta, Upatissa Pasine, and the Rahulovada (Bairat Rock Edict).

Vinayasamukkaseis, a text exalting the Vinaya.

Ariyavasani refers to the contentment of a monk in requisites, finding pleasure in development and abandoning.

Anagatabhayas are the five fears of the future for monks in the forest. They might be killed by men, animals, accidents, or bad food. Thinking of this danger, they become more energetic in their meditative practice.

Munigatha is praised for the recluse who goes alone to find calm, annihilating further existences, strong in understanding, virtue, and concentration.

The Mauneya Sutta praises calm and the detachment of recluseship.

The Rahulovada Sutta describes Buddha admonishing Rahula about conscious false speech.

The Upatissapasine Sutta recounts Sariputta asking Buddha many questions.

Conclusion

Asoka ruled for an estimated forty years. After his death, the Mauryan Dynasty lasted just fifty more years. His children, Venerable Mahinda and Sanghamitta played an important role in the spread of Buddhism by entering the Sangha and traveling to Sri Lanka to establish Buddhism there. Asoka appointed one of his sons, Kunala, as his successor. Asoka died in 232 BCE. The Mauryan dynasty ended during the rule of Brhadrata in 185 BCE. Without King Asoka's efforts to spread Buddhism to neighboring countries, the teachings of the Buddha would not have remained intact. *Sadhu, sadhu, sadhu for his gift of Dhamma.*

REFERENCES

- Ambedkar, B.R. 1996. *Bauddha Dharma O Darshan.* Mahabodhi Book Agency, Kolkata.

- Barua, Dipak Kumar. 2015. *Buddhist Philosophy.* Createspace Publishing, California, USA.

- Barua, Sukomal. *Bharate Bauddha Dharmer Itihas.* Bangladesh: Dhaka University, 1996.

- *Brainwave: A Multidisciplinary Journal* ,Vol 1, vol 2, vol 3, vol 4, vol 5.

- Brammachary, Pandit Silananda. *Mahasanti Mahaprem.* Kolkata, India: Maha Bodhi Book   Agency, 1996.

- Das, Asha. 2013. *Bauddha Darshan O Rabindranath.* India: Mahabodhi Book Agency, Kolkata-73.

- Das, Asha, 2014. *Indian Philosophy & Buddhism.* Mahabodhi Book Agency, Kolkata.

- Mahasthavir, Pandit Dharmadar. 1994. *Dhammapada,* Dharmadhar Bouddha Grantha Prakasani, Calcutta.

- Priya, Buddha Mahathero. 2016. *The Light of Peace*, 2nd ed. SUSWM, Kolkata.

- Sankrityayan, Mahapandita Rahul. 1989, *Buddhist Philosophy.* Moscow: Lenin University.

- Sen, Ranabrata, ed. 1968. *Dhammapada*, Haraf Prakasani, Kolkata.

- Tagore, Rabindranathi. 1984. *Maitri Bhavana O Bauddha Darshan.* Shantiniketan, India: Visva Bharati.

- Vivekananda, Swami. 1996. *Buddha O Bauddha Dharma, 8th ed.* West Bengal, India: Belur Math.

DR. BABASAHEB AMBEDKAR'S GREAT CONTRIBUTION OF BUDDHISM

Rutuja Siddharth Jondhale

Siddharth Hospital and Research Centre, New Mondha

Abstract

*B*ahujanahitāsutt and bahujanahitasuttavaṇṇanā are inherent, infinite, and dynamic in nature. The eternal relationship of the human mind is on a cosmological level, a consciousness level, and a physical level. The omniscience of Buddha, which *is pariyātidhammā, paṭipadādhammā*, and *paṭivedhadhamm*ā, are the great contributions of Buddhism that represent social revolution. Buddhist epistemology investigates the omniscience of the Buddha represented by his infinite knowledge.

B. R. Ambedkar

Bhimrao Ramji Ambedkar 1891–1956) was an Indian jurist, economist, social reformer, and political leader who headed the committee drafting the Constitution of India from the Constituent Assembly debates, where he served as Law and Justice Minister.

Contributions of Buddhism

Once the Blessed Lord was staying at Shravasti in Anathapindika's Arama where Sariputta was also staying. The Lord addressing the Brethren said:

Almsmen, be ye partakers not of the world's goods but of my doctrine; in my compassion for you all I am anxious to ensure this. Thus spoke the Lord, who thereupon rose and passed to his own cell. Sariputta remained behind and the brethren asked him to explain Nibbana. Then Sariputta in reply to the Brethren said, 'Brethren, know you that greed is vile, and vile is resentment. To shed this greed and this resentment, there is the Middle Way which gives us eyes to see and makes us know, leading us on to peace, insight, enlightenment and Nibbana. What is this Middle Way? It is naught but the Noble Eightfold Path of right outlook, right aims, right speech, right action, right means of livelihood, right effort, right mindfulness, and right concentration; this, almsmen is the Middle Way.'

Yes, sirs; anger is vile, and malevolence is vile, envy and jealousy are vile, niggardliness and avarice are vile, hypocrisy and deceit and arrogance are vile, inflation is vile, and indolence is vile. "For the shedding of inflation and indolence there is the Middle Way-giving us eyes to see, making us know, and leading us on to peace, insight, enlightenment. Nibbana which is naught but that Noble Eightfold Path. Thus spoke the reverend Sariputta-glad at heart, the almsmen rejoiced at what he had said (Rahula, 2007). [The Noble Eightfold Path by Walapola Sri Rahula, W.A. Howes Ltd., Sri Lanka, 2007.]

Contributions of Babasaheb Ambedkar on Buddhism Found in Writing and Speeches

Five precepts *surāmerayamajjapamādaṭṭhānā veramaṇī,pañcasīla*), abstention from killing living beings (*pāṇātipātā veramaṇī*), abstention from sexual misconduct (*kāmesumicchācāra veramaṇī*), abstention from alcoholic drink and intoxicants, abstention from telling lies *(musāvādā veramaṇī)*, and abstention from theft (*adinnādānā veramaṇī*). The Bahujanahitasuttavaṇṇanā way results in eternal purification of the metaphysical and holistic way of life which represents infinite *karuṇā*.

Conclusion

Bahujanahitāsutt and bahujanahitasuttavaṇṇanā are inherent and infinitely dynamic in nature. The eternal relationship of the human mind is on a cosmological level, consciousness level, and physical level. The omniscience of Buddha, which is pariyātidhammā, paṭipadādhammā, and paṭivedhadhammā, are the great contributions of Buddhism.

Gratitude

Great gratitude to our Dhamma Master Ven. Dr. Buddha Priya Mahathero.

REFERENCES

- Rahula, Walpola Sr. 2007. *The Noble Eightfold Path.* Sri Lanka: W.A.Howes, Ltd.

- Tripitaka

- Wikipedia

- Writing and Speeches: 1) Sermons on Nibbana, 2) What Is Nibbana

OMNISCIENCE OF THE BUDDHA & THE LAW OF PIETY

Deshana Siddharth Jondhale

Siddharth Hospital and Research Centre

New Mondha, Maharashtra, India

Abstract

*K*ing Piyadasi sends greeting to the Magadhan clergy and wishes them prosperity and good health, "Ye know, Reverend Sirs, how great is my respect for and devotion to the Buddha, the Law, and the Assembly of the Clergy." The famous Buddhist Triad, or triratna, "the law," *dhammasi,* means here the whole body of Buddhist doctrine, not only those principles of practical piety which are expounded in edicts addressed to the public.

The omniscience of the Buddha is expressed in the conditional relations with the law of piety (*paṭṭhāna*) and dependent origination (*paṭiccasamuppāda*). Conditional relations and infinite Buddhist cosmology are the correlation for the law of piety. The infinite nature of Abhidhamma is a representation of peace. The way of Abhidhamma and eternal purification of the metaphysical and holistic way for life represents infinite karuṇā and mettā.

Buddhist Law of Piety and the Metaphorical Use of Chakhu

The only authentic account of the reasons that induced Asoka to adopt the Buddhist Dharma or Law of Piety as the rule of his life and the foundation of public morality, is the above-quoted edict as being the best means of securing the happiness and welfare of his subjects and neighbors.

Correlation and Explanation of the Omniscience of Buddha

The law, *dhammasi,* means here the whole body of Buddhist doctrine, and not only those principles of practical piety which are expounded in the edicts addressed to the general public.

With the correlation between conditional relations with metaphorical use of *chakkhu*, a *sotāpanna* (stream-enterer) reflects the nature of human beings that can develop the great spiritual qualities within the mind. These are representations of infinite peace.

Infinite spiritual metaphysical consciousness: The first moment of attainment is termed the path of stream-entry. The person who experiences this is called a stream-winner (sotāpanna). This metaphor is representative of a deeper peace intercorrelates with the metaphorical chakku.

The infinite spiritual metaphysical consciousness can be experienced with the adaptation of pariyātidhammā, paṭipadādhammā, and paṭivedhadhammā in daily life. The Abhidhamma is dynamic in nature-this is the omniscience of the Buddha.

Correlation Between Omniscience of the Buddha and

Meditation

"For they all desire mastery over the senses and purity of mind. For pious acts and the practice of piety depend on the growth among men of compassion, liberality, truth, purity, gentleness, and goodness. Thus, said His Majesty King Piyadasi." This growth of piety among men has been affected by two means, namely, by pious regulations and by meditation. Of these two means, pious regulations are of small account, whereas meditation is of greater value.

Conclusion

The Law of Piety reflects the infinite nature of Abhidhamma which is a representation of peace and purification of the metaphysical and holistic way of life.

Gratitude

My Dear Great Brother, Venerable Dr. Buddha Priya Mahathero: *My deepest gratitude to you for your blessings, love, and compassion for me and for my Abhidhamma research work.*

REFERENCES

- Ambedkar, B.R., *The Buddha and His Dhamma*, 2019, Samyak Prakashan, New Delhi.

- Edict VII Imperfect Fulfilment of The Law, His Majesty King Priyadarsin desires that in all   places   men   of   all sects may abide.

- Smith, Vincent A. *Rulers Of India Asoka the Buddhist Emperor of India.*

- The Indian Civil Service, Edict V Censors of The Law of Piety, Edict II the Royal Example

- The Bhabra Edict (Probably the eighteenth year of the reign), the Bhabra Edict Address to the   Clergy   of Magadha, King Piyadasi Sends Greeting to The Magadhan

Clergy

- The Indian Civil Service, Edict V Censors of The Law of Piety Edict II the Royal Example,
- Tripitaka
- Wikipedia

TRACING THE FOOTPRINTS OF BUDDHA: FROM INDIA TO THE WORLD

Priyanka Barua

A Devotee, Howrah, West Bengal

The Scripture of the Saviour of the World,
Lord Buddha-Prince Siddartha styled on earth-
In Earth and Heavens and Hells Incomparable,
All-honoured, Wisest, Best, most Pitiful;
The Teacher of Nirvana and the Law.

- Edwin Arnold, The Light of Asia

*f*rom time immemorial religion has bound civilizations together. From the Harappan civilization to the modern era, the Indian subcontinent has seen the shift from worship of Mother Nature to the rise of Hinduism, from the rise of Jainism and Buddhism to the advent of Christianity and Islam and the birth of Sikhism. The Indian subcontinent has been home to various cultures and civilizations giving birth to different religious movements.

One such religion that was born in the heartland of India and later spread its wings worldwide is Buddhism, the extraordinary story of the Lord of Enlightenment or "the light of Asia" as Sir Edwin Arnold called him.

Born as Siddhartha Gautama in Lumbini to royal family of the Shakya clan, he could have led a life of luxury and died in peace, but he chose to conquer his insight, he chose to face his conscience, he chose to step out of luxury into the reality of pain, suffering, and death associated with old age. Buddha's time saw the rise of economic and political power struggle among the Janapadas along with strict orthodoxy of Brahminic rituals. Buddha sought liberation from this endless cycle of desire, greed, grief, and death. His Four Noble Truths explain the truth of suffering, the cause of suffering, the end of suffering and the path that leads to the end of suffering. This path is the Noble Eightfold Path that stresses right speech, right action, right thought, right livelihood, right concentration, right effort, right mindfulness, and right understanding. Buddha, through his *Madhyama Marg,* asked his followers to avoid the two extremes of indulgence in worldly pleasure and the practice of strict abstinence and asceticism.

Lord Buddha was not an omnipotent or omnipresent god, but a preacher who showed us the path to Nirvana or salvation. His first sermon, the "Dharmachakra Pravartana" or "Turning the Wheel of Dhamma" was in the Deer Park in Sarnath, Varanasi. Buddha traveled extensively through Uruvela to Rajgriha and met King Bimbisara and he, along with his followers, accepted the new order initiated by the Buddha. Buddha visited Kapilavastu, Sravasti and several Janapadas to preach his doctrine of peace, compassion, and brotherhood.

However, it was 200 years after his death that the Buddha was introduced to the world outside. It was King Ashoka of the Mauryan Dynasty, who, through his missionaries, spread Buddhism to the Far East and Far West. It was Buddha's teachings that forced the powerful and ruthless King Ashoka to adopt Buddhism after one of the bloodiest battles in history, the Kalinga war. Ashoka renounced violence and embraced Ahimsa after this war. His policy of Dhamma incorporated Buddha's teachings. It was a moral code of conduct with ethical principles and humanitarian ideals promoting universal brotherhood and peaceful coexistence.

Ashoka built around 84,000 stupas to place Buddha's relics. He constructed the first temple complex of the Seat of Awakening, Mahabodhi Mahavihara in Bodh Gaya. He also built the famous Dhameka Stupa in Sarnath and the marvelous Sanchi Stupa. However, the most significant step taken by him was sending his missionaries to the east and to the west. He sent missionaries to countries like Ceylon, Greece, Thailand, and Egypt, to name a few. Ashoka sent his son Mahendra and daughter Sanghamitra to Ceylon to spread Buddhism and even planted a part of the sacred Bodhi tree over there. His dispatch of Buddhist missionaries marked one of the historic efforts in propagating Buddhism to the world.

Another ruler who patronized Buddhism was the Kushan king, Kanishka. In his era, Mahayana Buddhism came into vogue and so did idol worship. Kanishka's conquests and patronage of Buddhism were crucial in the development of the Silk Road and the transmission of Buddhism from Gandhara to China. His reign saw the rise of Gandhara and Mathura schools of art, heavily influenced by the Buddhist traditions. With the influence of the Kushans, Buddhism spread not only eastward to China, but also westward to Afghanistan. One such glaring example still standing tall is of the Bamiyan Buddha built during the fifth century. They are two colossal statues of Buddha, once the tallest standing Buddhas of the world. However, now they stand in ruins as a victim of destruction by the Taliban.

Buddhism was propagated throughout the world by not only the great rulers, but also by the many travelers who visited India in search of the true knowledge of awakening and enlightenment. With the advent of Chinese travelers like Fa-Hien, Hiuen Tsang and I-Tsing the study of Buddhism reached new heights. Buddhism gained prominence in China with the valuable scriptures and manuscripts that they carried back to their country. By the seventh century Buddhism gradually spread to Java and Sumatra by the Shailendra Dynasty. It was during this period that the marvelous Borobudur Stupa was constructed.

Buddhism has evolved through ages. The first Buddhist Council held immediately after the *Mahaparinirvana* of Buddha to the fourth Buddhist Council held during the first century CE, Buddhism changed its course and splintered into different schools in different regions of India, from the southern *Theravada* school in Sri Lanka to *Sarvastivada* tradition in Kashmir. The Theravada emphasized attaining liberation through one's own efforts. It emerged from Sri Lanka to countries like Cambodia, Thailand, Laos, and Burma. Another school of Buddhist practice initiated in India and mostly developed in Tibet during the seventh and eighth century was the *Vajrayana* or the "Thunderbolt Vehicle." It is also known as Tantric Buddhism, practiced mostly along the Himalayan settlements bordering Tibet, and flourished by the legendary Buddhist mystic Guru Padmasambhava or Guru Rinpoche.

Today Buddhism has become one of the dominant religions of the world with over 500 million followers comprising roughly 7 percent of world population. Buddhism has indeed come a long way from its roots. Devotees have resorted to different routes of devotion. Yet what binds us together across the globe is that one man, that one enlightened one, the Buddha. Buddhism, today, has evolved into a multicultural, multilingual, global religion. The task of spreading Buddhism started by Ashoka has culminated into a reality and the seeds of Buddha's teachings have germinated across continents, contributing towards universal compassion, peace and above all, *Nirvana.*

THE PEACEFUL MESSAGE
OF THE BUDDHA

Meditation Master Dr. Buddha Priya Mahathero

General Secretary of SUSWM and BSBM, Kolkata, India

Email: psuswm@ymail.com

Namo Buddhaya

*B*uddhism is not just a religion of the past or a mere faith as many have thought, but a time-tested scientific religion and philosophy which, in the context of the present world situation, is more relevant today than ever before for establishing world peace.

Abstract

For us in India, the land of Buddha's birth, Buddhism is an outstanding representation of our religious tradition-a tradition of peace and harmony. Humanism, which was a hallmark of Buddha's teachings, crossed all racial and national barriers. The master aimed at the development of a new kind of free man, intent on working out his own future, with reliance on one's own self, *attadipa*. But today, more than even before, we're suffering from an exhaustion of spirit, an increase of egoism, individual and collective, which makes the ideal of a world society difficult to achieve.

Buddha has been a great force for peace in the world. Buddha's policy of peace, self-sacrifice, kindness, and charity molded the lives of numerous saints in medieval India, while in modern India too, some great leaders like Gandhi and Nehru have undoubtedly been guided by Buddha's teachings. The declared foreign policy of India was based on Five Precepts (*panchashila*), in itself a Buddhist term, allows for the possibility of peaceful co-existence between people of different ideologies.

In the present, no less than in the past, Buddhism implies peace, implying a state of mind (*metta*). The message of Buddhism and the principles on which it rests have assumed a new significance in today's world. Even the peace of which U.N.O. speaks is but an indication that the entire world (Morgan 1956, 12) is gradually veering around the belief embodied in the religion of the Buddha.

Buddhism has an intimate association with the concept of peace. In its long history, we find hardly any evidence of violence, killings or religious hatred. "Buddhism wields only one sword, the sword of wisdom and recognizes only one enemy, ignorance." This is, indeed, the testimony of history.

In India, Buddha's policy of peace, self-sacrifice, kindness, and charity not only influenced people in general but also rulers who made it the basis of their state policy. It molded the lives of many saints in medieval India, while in modern period too, leaders like Gandhi and Nehru were undoubtedly guided by Buddha's teachings. The declared foreign policy of India was based on five precepts, *panchashila*, a Buddhist term which allows for the possibility of peaceful co-existence between people of different ideologies.

World peace, today, appears to be a myth, a mirage. However, it is equally true that despite diversity of race, religion, ideology and so forth, people all over the world are near unanimous in their basic wish for peace and happiness. Today, at the threshold of the twenty-first century the world is in dire need of peace which should produce harmony, universal brotherhood, love, compassion, forbearance, equanimity, and breed solace in interpersonal relationships. International humanitarianism, nonviolence and world peace are a foremost necessity of today.

The problem of peace-whether individual or social-is essentially a problem of mind. It's the positive state of the human mind which comprehends joy and happiness which are borne out of selfless love for all sentient beings of the universe. Man hankers after peace because happiness is the ultimate goal of all living beings, and in the quest for happiness, intelligent man finds that it is not available as long as one's mind is not at peace.

In the strife-torn world of today, the message of Buddha holds great relevance. He wanted to lift, not only man, but the entire human race above and beyond the fear, ignorance and isolation which beset him in his path of life. As for its message of peace, it pervades the whole Buddhist tradition. Buddha realized that peace would come only when man is happy. He wanted man to get rid of all malice, hatred, indulgence in lower desires and evil thoughts. He wanted to substitute these with good thoughts, worthy desires, feelings of charity and compassion, and an attitude of serenity and composure. Let men purify their thoughts and desires and complete happiness will be theirs. Such a thought effort will, then, lead to universal peace.

As a social code, Buddhism leads us to peace, understanding, and integration. Buddha tried to inculcate in his followers the sense of service and understanding with love and compassion by separating man from passion and elevating humanistic tendencies in man with the help of morality, *karuna,* and *samata.*

Peace and integrity are the central theme of Buddhism. It is indispensable for world peace as a way of securing integral growth and stability. Buddha's chief motto was that not only all members of the Buddhist order, but rather all subjects of state, must achieve the ethical perfection and moral integrity which only will produce peace both within as well as outside the state.

In the changing world of today, Buddhism has a great deal to contribute to establishing peace. It provides for a revolutionary doctrine of peace by way of a concept of commonwealth of Dharma. Though the message of peace is strewn all over in Buddhism, we may make a passing reference to some of the early Buddhist scriptures, as well as later Mahayana philosophical and literary works, which contain specific references to peace. Among the earlier works, the Kimsita Sutra of the Cullavagga states that whosoever practices the Dhamma in accordance with Buddha's teachings and attains the essence of knowledge through meditation is established in peace. The three sutras of the Mahavagga (Sundarikabhadvaja, Magha , and Salla), most of the sutras of the Atthaka Vagga, and the complete chapter of the Parayanavagga delineate the Buddhist conception of peace as one's individual attainment of complete mental freedom by one's endeavor of renouncing craving, all philosophical doctrines, and religious ceremonies. Similarly, later Mahayana works depict the Bodhisattva as a personification of Mahakaruna. Asvaghosha's Vajrasuchi aptly shows how Mahayana acaryas tried to rise above the distinctions of caste, color, and creed, in accordance with Buddha's teachings, so as to establish peace within the state.

In this paper it is proposed to refer briefly to the concept of *ahimsa* or nonviolence enunciated by Buddha which went a long way in promoting the concept of peace. Subsequently, we propose to examine how this concept of peace is reflected in two very prominent Buddhist works, namely Saddharmapundarikasutra or the Lotus of the True Law and Kalachakra Tantra or the Wheel of Time. However, before we do that it will be worthwhile analyzing, briefly, the historical background which paved the way for the rise of Buddhism in the sixth century BC.

In order to understand the significance of peace in the context of early Buddhism, it is necessary to traverse the historical background of the rise of Buddhism. The age of Buddhism was an age when, as a result of the development of the forces of production, the northern regions of India witnessed the rise of ruthless state powers on the ruins of tribal societies. Trade and war were creating unheard of miseries in the lives of the people while the greed for private property knew no bounds. Nevertheless, the productive forces were not developed enough to provide plenty for all. Rather, the further development of the productive forces which alone could lead to eventual happiness must have then presupposed a more ruthless force of exploitation and all the miseries it entailed. Simultaneously, the Gangetic Basin in the sixth century BC witnessed the emergence of new classes leading to lot of social tensions, while in the religious sphere arose so many sects of considerable appeal and prominence with their diverse philosophies, "a bewildering cluster of the frustrated ideas."

In responding to such a situation, the Buddha was merely acting as an unconscious tool of history, and Buddhism from its very inception was destined to become perhaps the biggest socio-religious movement in Indian history.

In formulating the theoretical basis of his Dhamma, Buddha looked upon the suffering of his age as a sickness, a disease. The *arya satyas*, noble truths which he pronounced were concerned with the suffering and formulated in a time that a witnessed the state of power and property. In order to bring peace to the afflicted, Buddha raised the concrete material sufferings of his fellow beings to a universal principle of eternal suffering, a kind of ideal or metaphysical suffering. With such an explanation, the actual miseries arising from the new social conditions paled into insignificance. The cause of misery, found in the very craving, was for existence. Buddha also came out with a message of deliverance from misery, proclaiming that suffering could be overcome and there was a definite way out for that. He further argued that the real cause of the actual suffering was to be sought somewhere outside the concrete material world, otherwise people would have taken a recourse of violence instead. The ultimate cause of all human suffering was traced to ignorance. The problem was solved simply by removing it from the realm of reality.

The core of Buddhism, the Noble Eightfold Path, appears to have been formulated to bring happiness and peace not only to the individuals but to society at large. The first step, proper vision, helps man in quenching the desire (root cause of all sorrow) and leads to the path of peace. The second step, proper aims, deters one from coveting wealth and power at the expense of others or indulging in senses and luxury and through proper design equips man to love others and increase their happiness. The third step, proper speech (truthful, conducive to eternal friendship, endearing and measured), exhorts one to avoid misuse of the tongue lest it may lead to violence and killings. The fourth step, proper action, advises one not to indulge in actions such as killing, theft, adultery leading to disaster, but rather to such positive deeds as would lead to the benefit of others. Similarly, other steps in the Eightfold Path also exhort us to remove evils from our mind, generate good thoughts to produce harmony and happiness in society.

Buddha not only prescribed a code of conduct for both the lay followers and the monks, but even ventured to pronounce new duties for the absolute monarch, which project "a startling Modern view of political economy."

Beside other things, it advises the ruler to tackle banditry and strife and other social evils like poverty and unemployment by proper means, to utilize surplus accumulation for the public works and thus ensure peace and harmony in the kingdom.

The doctrine of Buddha was eminently fitted to the needs of a rapidly evolving society. The Buddha's attitude to the injustices of the caste system made a fervent appeal to the people. Of the contemporary prophets, Buddha alone "could offer to the people of his times the illusion of liberty, equality and fraternity, which, as the inevitable result of the laws of social advance, were being trampled and undermined in reality."

The age of the Buddha saw the most momentous social upheavals in the Gangetic Valley, the transition from tribe to state, the changed composition of the army (without a tribal basis), a new set of institutions (mortgage, interest, usury), and emerging merchant classes with concomitant social vices characteristic of commercialism. Amidst the tension generated by these, what was required was some sort of substitute for the lost tribal value of liberty, equality, fraternity. It was Buddha who provided a substitute and became extremely popular.

In different suttas, Buddha talks about the insatiable greed of the rich. The new realities which he saw were appalling to him. The same greed for riches and power characterizes the political history of the age. Numerous cases of patricide as recorded in the history of Magadha and Kosala were manifestations of the new values that followed the rise of state power and collapse of tribal morality. In a world torn to pieces by the new forces of tyranny, oppression, and greed, of lust and hatred, Buddha's message of peace, *ahimsa*, compassion, amity and harmony and his emphasis on the moral values proved timely and had tremendous appeal for the masses.

Ahimsa or Nonviolence

Buddhism is a gospel of peace and nonviolence. Nonviolence is a way of life devoid of all extremes of passion like anger, enmity, pleasure, and pain. True peace emanates from nonviolence which is a rational and mighty force. The practice of nonviolence is life-affirming which contributes to human unity, progress, and peace. Nonviolence teaches one to live in harmony with others and with oneself. It requires adherence to high standards of truth and self-control.

Buddhism is considered to be a practical religion of peace and nonviolence. The four Brahma-viharas, friendliness, compassion, joy, and equanimity which are ingredients of Right Mindfulness tend to promote global welfare. Further, the Bodhisattva ideal based on an unselfish and sacrificing spirit, the compassionate and benevolent attitude of the Buddha towards the whole of mankind, and the principles of ahimsa or nonviolence, forbearance and a humanitarian outlook all tend to promote peace.

No one can afford to overlook the nonviolent strategy and

social policy instituted by the Buddha. The Buddhist Sangha is a true army of nonviolence. Buddha probably realized that one individual taming one's mind was not enough, but effort was to be made to tame the minds of millions of men. Hence, he decided to create an army of men wearing orange robes with shaven heads-an army of nonviolent warriors whose battle was to conquer the self.

The principle of nonviolence projects an ideal of universal peace. Buddhists, in the twenty-first century, have a responsibility to rediscover how their tradition of ahimsa, love. and compassion can help individuals realize peace, not only in their own life, but also in the world community.

Saddharmapundarika Sutra or Lotus of the True Law

The Buddhist ideal of peace is beautifully illustrated in Saddharmapundarika Sutra or the Lotus of the True Law, one of the most important of all Mahayana scriptures, setting forth the doctrine of the One Vehicle and the eternal Buddha. The sutra teaches an ethical path which is the way of the Boddhisattva-a life of creative altruism leading to ultimate peace.

The Lotus, with its countless teachings, embodies an ideology of peace. The best foundation for world peace is universal responsibility towards equitable distribution of natural resources and thorough concern for future generations which can make the world one, a pure and peaceful land. In the Lotus Sutra, absolutely nothing is excluded from this teaching-mind, body, individual, society, mountain, river, tree, grass, bird, fish, animal, or seeds-everything will be saved. The breadth and boundlessness of the Lotus Sutra is overwhelming. It is, undoubtedly, a profound teaching on peace.

The Lotus of the True Law tells the story of Devadatta (Chapter XII), a disciple and also a cousin of Buddha, who subsequently defied the Buddha and broke away from Buddha's community of disciples. He indulged in crimes of murder, slandering the Dhamma, causing dissensions among Buddha's disciples and even attempting to kill Buddha on various occasions. Comparing the evil deeds of Devadatta with that of Buddha who endured them, we learn many valuable lessons. The story conveys a range of overt expressions of both violence and nonviolence and one can easily make out as to which one is more powerful.

The spirit of the Lotus does not aim solely at the salvation of individuals or awakening them to the truth, but ultimately aims at changing the whole society. This is symbolized by the words "to purify the Buddha land" which appear frequently in the "Lotus." The Lotus Sutra asserts that in order for man to become truly happy, in addition to individual enlightenment and happiness in one's individual life, one must also seek to purify the nation (society), thus going a step further. Chapter XI of the Lotus, "Beholding the Precious Stupa," exhorts a person to make efforts not to escape from actuality but rather to positively wrestle with and strive to purify it. Another important lesson one derives from the chapter is that the person who intends to make this world peaceful should directly touch the sufferings of the ordinary people in actual society. One can't serve others by idealism alone but must grapple with actual problems.

"The Divine Power of the Tathagata" (Chapter XXI), a symbolic recapitulation of the ideas of the "Lotus" explains that Buddha reveals divine power and shows various mysteries of miraculous phenomenon, all of which symbolize the truth that everyone is one. The phenomenon "One Buddhaland" occurring here means the formation of a world federation which we must try to translate into action.

The Lotus Sutra describes the actions of people working for the peace of humanity in terms of bodhisattvas of various kinds. Among them, the Bodhisattva Never Disparaging (Chapter XX) provides a model of nonviolent dialogue. He believes in and respects human dignity to the maximum extent. In essence, what Sakyamuni was trying to achieve by appearing in this world was the optimum way of life for both the self and others. Similarly, "Bodhisattvas from the Earth" (Chapter XV) appear as those who will disseminate the spirit of the Lotus Sutra in the future. It is predicted that they'll appear together with the philosophy of respect for the dignity of life in the evil age of five impurities, the Latter Day of the Law.

In our terms, the bodhisattvas appearing in the Lotus Sutra can be seen as representing ordinary people striving to create a culture of peace. The heart of their endeavors is respect for the dignity of life. Their principal tool is nonviolent, compassionate dialogue, and each one of them manifests his or her distinctive characteristics while working for the achievement of this goal.

Chapter II of the sutra, "Expedient Means," clearly states that Buddhas appear in this world for the purpose of revealing to sentient beings the universal life (Buddha nature) in each one of them. Their aim is to open and show living beings wisdom, awaken them to it, and cause them to become one with it. This glorifies the dignity of life and helps sentient beings to be as good as they are capable of being. Again, it is held that whereas ignorance evokes evil energy creating schisms, good energy becomes manifest by the true nature of all phenomena and the Buddha's nature becomes compassion, trust, wisdom, courage, and justice. And when all things, including humanity, reveal the good nature and are united in solidarity, the essential dignity of life based on the law of dependent origination is made manifest. It is only under such circumstances that we may strive to create a culture of peace, characterized by nonviolence, compassion, trust, and hope.

The Buddhist ideal culture of peace is described in Chapter V, "The Parable of the Medicinal Herbs" of the Lotus Sutra. It is stated here that in nature grow a great diversity of plants and trees. Receiving the equal blessings of earth and rain, they grow and blossom, each manifesting its own characteristics. This text, in which earth and rain are metaphors for Shakyamuni's impartial teachings and plants represent living beings, skillfully describes the nature of the culture of peace. "In social terms, the parable indicates how diverse cultures can preserve their distinctive natures while co-existing peacefully."

Kalachakra: Wheel of Time

Kalachakra, one of the greatest divisions of Tantric Buddhism, in Sanskrit means "Tantra of the Wheel of Time." Kalachakra is part of an elaborate system. It's a Tantric teaching that Tibetans consider especially useful for eliminating or at least reducing war and is full of positive effects. It is reported that in 1953 His Holiness Dalai Lama received the Kalachakra Initiation1 from Ling Rinpoche. This is one of the most important initiations in the Tantric tradition with special significance for world peace. Subsequently, His Holiness has given the Kalachakra Initiation at different places in India and abroad, with the motive to promote world peace.

However, to achieve genuine world peace, we have first to create inner peace. This is only possible when we reduce our negative thoughts and increase positive attitudes by developing love and compassion, patience and understanding among human beings. A universal humanitarian approach to world problems, then, appears to be the only sound basis for world peace.

Kalachakra came to be developed for the welfare and prosperity of all beings and for peace at the individual and global level. But as long as we suffer from mental distortions as attachment and anger, peace will be impossible to achieve. Kalachakra helps the initiated to overcome such mental distortions and develop a state of mind to enable them to achieve peace, both within and without. Such a harmony of exterior and interior is said to be possible only through the study of Kalachakra.

The Kalachakra initiation is a workshop on a grand scale to make an earnest effort by both the teacher and the disciple to awaken the Buddha nature, the innate goodness, by the combined force of teaching, prayer, blessing, devotion, mantra, yoga, and meditation. It is an effort by every participant to try to discover true and permanent peace for the sake of all others.12 [Wikipedia] The Kalachakra Initiation, the highest form of Tibetan Buddhist Tantric practice, leads one to complete enlightenment attaining the Bodhicitta and realization of shunyata in one's own lifetime.

The only way a lasting peace could be established is by cultivating enlightened peace in the minds of the people. The Kalachakra is considered to be a unique and practical step in this direction.

Kalachakra creates the right aspiration of a Bodhisattva wishing to become an enlightened being in order to help all other beings. The Kalachakra practice is the Buddhist means of achieving Bodhicitta and becoming the Buddha in one's own lifetime. The Bodhicitta is the intuitive feeling, unclouded by selfishness, anger, or fear.

To conclude, one may say that Buddha's teaching of overcoming evil helped humanity in achieving peace. It had tremendous impact on the general and social being of the society thereby contributing to amity and social harmony. It revived the spirit of social solidarity by putting an end to social conflict. The noble mission of the Buddha helped not only India but also southeastern and Far eastern countries to create conditions for justice, political and socio-economic stability, fraternity, peace, and social harmony.

The message of Buddha, and the principles on which it rests, have assumed a new significance in today's world. Even the peace of which UNO speaks is but an indication that the world is gradually veering around the beliefs embodied in the religion of the Buddha.

It is the essence of Buddhism that:

Sabba Papassa Akaranam

Kusalassa upasampoda

Sacitta pariyodapanam

Etam Buddhanosasanam

* * *

Avoid all evil deeds,

Cultivate the wholesome,

purify one's own mind-

this is the universal teaching of the Buddha.

Bhabato sabba mangalam

May all sentient beings be happy, peaceful, and liberated.

REFERENCES

- Bodhi, Bhikkhu, *The Living Message of the Dhammapada*, 1993, Buddhist Publication Society, Kandy, Sri Lanka.

- Brammachary, Pandit Silananda. 2011. *Mahasanti Mahaprem, pg.77*. Kolkata: Maha Bodhi B o o k Agency.

- Buddharakkhita, Acharya, trans. *The Dhammapada: The Buddha's Path to Wisdom*. Buddhanet.net, https://www. accesstoinsight.org/tipitaka/kn/dhp/dhp.intro.budd.html

- Dhammananda, Venerable K. Sri. *Buddhism in the Eye of Intellectuals*, Taiwan: The Corporate Body of Buddha Educational Foundation.

- Mahajan, Silabhadra Rinpoche. 2002. *Kalachakara*. Darjeeling: Bodhi Publications. 34, 112.

- Morgan, Kenneth W., ed. 1956. *Path of the Buddha: Buddhism Interpreted by Buddhists*: New Y o r k : Kessinger Publishing Company.

- Norman, Alexander. 2020. *The Dalai Lama: An Extraordinary Life*, New Delhi: Harper Collins.

- Pandit, Jyotipal Mahathero, 1988. *Karmatattva*. Dhaka: Kumilla Book Publisher, 32.

- Priya, Buddha Mahathero. 2016. *The Light of Peace*, 2nd ed. Kolkata: SUSWM.

- Saksana, Rakesh, *Buddhism and Its Message of Peace*, Hindistan, India, www.ayk.gov.tr.

THE GALLERY PICTURES
OF KOLKATA

Buddhist Studies Conference, Siddharth United Social Welfare
Mission, Kolkata, West Bengal, India, 2nd July, 2023

1. At the gate of Siddharth United Social Welfare Mission

2. Dr. Buddha Priya Mahathero greeting
Vietnamese-American group

3. *Distinguished Speakers*

4. *Offer flowers and Dharma Bands to Guests*

5. Offer flowers to Ven. Dr. Bhikṣuṇī TN Gioi Huong

*6. Offer flowers and Dharma bands
to Vietnamese-American group*

7. Whole view of the seminar

8. From right: Ven. TN Gioi Huong, Rev. Tri Minh, Rev. Duc Tri, Rev. Vien Nhuan and Rev. Vien Bao

*9. Offer flowers and Dharma bands
to Vietnamese-American group*

10. Dr. Buddha Priya Mahathero with his welcome note

11. Dr. Buddha Priya Mahathero
and Ven. Dr. Bhikṣuṇī TN Gioi Huong

12. Banner introduction of Ven. Dr. Bhikṣuṇī TN Gioi Huong

13. Ven. Dr. Bhikṣuṇī Gioi Huong presents her paper

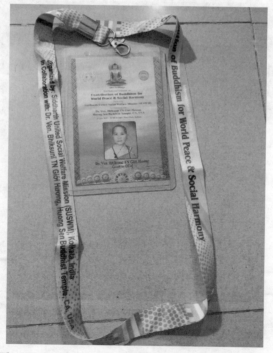

14. The Tag of Ven. Dr. Bhikṣuṇī TN Gioi Huong

15. Bhikṣuṇī Trí Minh presents her paper

*16. Ven. Dr. Bhikṣuṇī TN Gioi Huong
receives her rewards such as*

17. Ven. Dr. Bhikṣuṇī TN Gioi Huong receives gift

18. Bảo Anh Lạc book gift

19. The gift bags of book for offering

20. Donations to Sangha

21. Gift to Monks

22. Vietnamese group offering gifts to Monastics

23. Offering Gift to Speakers

24. Offering Gift to Scholars

25. Offering Gift to Dr. Buddha Priya Mahathero

26. The group of Speakers

27. Group photo

28. Ven. Dr. Bhikṣuṇī TN Gioi Huong
at the Kolkata seminar hall

29. Huong Sen Charity and Pilgrimage Banner

30. At the charity, Bhikṣuṇī TN Gioi Huong
read the Take Refuge at Triple Gem in English and
Dr. Buddha Priya Mahathero translated into Bangle
language for the local people

*31. At the charity, Bhikṣuṇī TN Tri Minh
guides the mindfulness in English and Dr. Buddha
Priya Mahathero translated into translated into Bangle
language for the local people*

32. Charity at Siddharth United Social Welfare Mission

33. Sharing rice and food to the local poor villagers

34. The sweats on the face

35. Indian women are happy to receive the gift

36. The group smiling after charity

*37. The memory photo at the office
of Dr. Buddha Priya Mahathero*

*38. Dr. Buddha Priya Mahathero
and Ven. Dr. Bhikṣuṇī TN Gioi Huong*

39. The Buddha hall of Rishra Jatavana Buddhist Temple, Kolkata, West Bengal

40. At the front of Rishra Jatavana Buddhist Temple, Kolkata, West Bengal

41. Great Social Service Award 2023 from Siddharth
United Social Welfare Mission

42. International Seminar Contribution of Buddhism For
World Peace & Social Harmony

BẢO ANH LẠC BOOKSHELF

1.1. THE VIETNAMESE BOOKS

1. *Bồ-tát và Tánh Không Trong Kinh Tạng Pali và Đại Thừa* (Boddhisattva and Sunyata in the Early and Developed Buddhist Traditions), Thích Nữ Giới Hương, Delhi-7: Tủ Sách Bảo Anh Lạc, 2005. Tổng Hợp Tp HCM Publishing: the 2nd & 3rd reprint in 2008 & 2010.

2. *Ban Mai Xứ Ấn* (The Dawn in India), (3 tập), Thích Nữ Giới Hương, Delhi-7: Tủ Sách Bảo Anh Lạc, 2005; Văn Hóa Sài Gòn Publishing: the 2nd, 3rd and 4th reprint in 2006, 2008 & 2010.

3. *Vườn Nai – Chiếc Nôi* (Phật Giáo Deer Park–The Cradle of Buddhism), Thích Nữ Giới Hương, Delhi-7: Tủ Sách Bảo Anh Lạc, 2005. Phương Đông Publishing: the 2nd, 3rd and 4th reprint in 2006, 2008 & 2010.

4. *Quy Y Tam Bảo và Năm Giới* (Take Refuge in Three Gems and Keep the Five Precepts), Thích Nữ Giới Hương, Tủ Sách Bảo Anh Lạc, Wisconsin, USA, 2008.

5. Phương Đông Publishing: the 2nd, 3rd and 4th reprint in 2010, 2016 &2018.

6. *Vòng Luân Hồi* (The Cycle of Life), Thích Nữ Giới Hương, Phương Đông Publishing: Tủ Sách Bảo Anh Lạc, 2008. Văn Hóa Sài Gòn Publishing: the 2nd, 3rd and 4th reprint in 2010, 2014 & 2016.

7. *Hoa Tuyết Milwaukee* (Snowflake in Milwaukee), Thích Nữ Giới Hương, Văn Hoá Sài gòn Publishing: Tủ Sách Bảo Anh Lạc, 2008.

8. *Luân Hồi trong Lăng Kính Lăng Nghiêm* (The Rebirth in

Śūraṅgama Sūtra), Thích Nữ Giới Hương, Văn Hóa Sài gòn Publishing: Tủ Sách Bảo Anh Lạc, 2008. Publishing Phương Đông: the 2nd, 3rd and 4th reprint in 2012, 2014 &2016.

9. *Nghi Thức Hộ Niệm, Cầu Siêu* (The Ritual for the Deceased), Thích Nữ Giới Hương, Delhi-7: Eastern Book Linkers, 2008.

10. *Quan Âm Quảng Trần* (The Commentary of Avalokiteśvara Bodhisattva), Thích Nữ Giới Hương, Tổng Hợp Publishing: Tủ Sách Bảo Anh Lạc, 2010. Publishing Phương Đông: the 2nd, 3rd, 4th & 5 reprint in 2010, 2014, 2016 & 2018.

11. *Nữ Tu và Tù Nhân Hoa Kỳ* (A Nun and American Inmates), Thích Nữ Giới Hương, Văn Hóa Sài gòn Publishing: Tủ Sách Bảo Anh Lạc, 2010. Hồng Đức Publishing: the 2nd, 3rd, 4th, 5th & 6th reprint in 2011, 2014, 2016, 2018 & 2020.

12. *Nếp Sống Tỉnh Thức của Đức Đạt Lai Lạt Ma Thứ XIV* (The Awakened Mind of the 14th Dalai Lama), 2 tập, Thích Nữ Giới Hương, Hồng Đức Publishing: Tủ Sách Bảo Anh Lạc, năm 2012. The 2nd, 3rd and 4th reprint in 2010, 2016 &2018.

13. *A-Hàm: Mưa pháp chuyển hóa phiền não* (*Agama – A Dharma Rain transforms the Defilement*), 2 tập, Thích Nữ Giới Hương, Hồng Đức Publishing: Tủ Sách Bảo Anh Lạc, năm 2012. The 2nd, 3rd and 4th reprint in 2010, 2016 &2018.

14. *Góp Từng Hạt Nắng Perris* (Collection of Sunlight in Perris), Thích Nữ Giới Hương, Hồng Đức Publishing: Tủ Sách Bảo Anh Lạc. 2014.

15. *Pháp Ngữ của Kinh Kim Cang* (The Key Words of Vajracchedikā-Prajñāpāramitā-Sūtra), Thích Nữ Giới Hương, Hồng Đức Publishing: Tủ Sách Bảo Anh Lạc, năm 2014. The 2nd, 3rd and 4th reprint in 2015, 2016 &2018.

16. *Tập Thơ Nhạc Nắng Lăng Nghiêm* (Songs and Poems of Śūraṅgama Sunlight), Thích Nữ Giới Hương, Hồng Đức Publishing: Tủ Sách Bảo Anh Lạc. 2014.

17. *Nét Bút Bên Song Cửa* (Reflections at the Temple Window), Thích Nữ Giới Hương, Hồng Đức Publishing: Tủ Sách Bảo

Anh Lạc. 2018.

18. *Máy Nghe MP3 Hương Sen* (Hương Sen Digital Mp3 Radio Speaker): Các Bài Giảng, Sách, Bài viết và Thơ Nhạc của Thích Nữ Giới Hương (383/201 bài), Hương Sen Temple. 2019.

19. *DVD Giới Thiệu về Chùa Hương Sen*, USA (Introduction on Huong Sen Temple). Hương Sen Press Publishing. Thích Nữ Giới Hương & Phú Tôn. 2019.

20. *Ni Giới Việt Nam Hoằng Pháp tại Hoa Kỳ* (Sharing the Dharma - Vietnamese Buddhist Nuns in the United States), Thích Nữ Giới Hương, Hồng Đức Publishing. 2020.

21. *Tuyển Tập 40 Năm Tu Học & Hoằng Pháp của Ni sư Giới Hương* (Forty Years in the Dharma: A Life of Study and Service—Venerable Bhikṣuṇī Giới Hương), Thích Nữ Viên Quang, TN Viên Nhuận, TN Viên Tiến, and TN Viên Khuông, Xpress Print Publishing, USA. 2020.

22. *Tập Thơ Nhạc Lối Về Sen Nở* (*Songs and Poems of Lotus Blooming on the Way*), Thích Nữ Giới Hương, Hồng Đức Publishing. 2020.

23. *Nghi Thức Công Phu Khuya – Thần Chú Thủ Lăng Nghiêm* (Śuraṅgama Mantra), Thích Nữ Giới Hương biên soạn, Hương Sen Press, USA. 2021.

24. *Nghi Thức Cầu An – Kinh Phổ Môn* (The Universal Door Sūtra), Thích Nữ Giới Hương biên soạn, Hương Sen Press, USA. 2021.

25. *Nghi Thức Cầu An – Kinh Dược Sư* (The Medicine Buddha Sūtra), Thích Nữ Giới Hương biên soạn, Hương Sen Press, USA. 2021.

26. *Nghi Thức Sám Hối Hồng Danh* (The Sūtra of Confession at many Buddha Titles), Thích Nữ Giới Hương biên soạn, Hương Sen Press, USA. 2021.

27. *Nghi Thức Công Phu Chiều – Mông Sơn Thí Thực* (The Ritual Donating Food to Hungry Ghosts), Thích Nữ Giới Hương biên soạn, Hương Sen Press, USA. 2021.

28. *Khóa Tịnh Độ – Kinh A Di Đà* (The Amitabha Buddha Sūtra), Thích Nữ Giới Hương biên soạn, Hương Sen Press, USA. 2021.

29. *Nghi Thức Cúng Linh và Cầu Siêu* (The Rite for Deceased and Funeral Home), Thích Nữ Giới Hương biên soạn, Hương Sen Press, USA. 2021.

30. *Nghi Lễ Hàng Ngày - 50 Kinh Tụng và các Lễ Vía trong Năm* (The Daily Chanting Rituals and Annual Ceremonies), Thích Nữ Giới Hương biên soạn, Hương Sen Press, USA. 2021.

31. *Hương Đạo Trong Đời 2022* (Tuyển tập 60 Bài Thi trong Cuộc Thi Viết Văn Ứng Dụng Phật Pháp 2022 - A Collection of Writings on the Practicing of Buddhism in Daily Life in the Writing Contest 2022), Thích Nữ Giới Hương biên soạn, Hồng Đức Publisher. 2022.

32. *Hương Pháp 2022* (Tuyển Tập Các Bài Thi Trúng Giải Cuộc Thi Viết Văn Ứng Dụng Phật Pháp 2022 - A Collection of the Winning Writings on the Practicing of Buddhism in Daily Life in the Writing Contest 2022) Thích Nữ Giới Hương biên soạn, Hồng Đức Publisher. 2022.

33. *Giới Hương - Thơm Ngược Gió Ngàn*, Nguyên Hà. XNB Hương Sen. USA. 2023.

34. *Pháp Ngữ Kinh Hoa Nghiêm* (2 tập). Thích Nữ Giới Hương. NXB Hương Sen. USA. 2023.

35. *Tinh Hoa Kinh Hoa Nghiêm*. Thích Nữ Giới Hương. NXB Hương Sen. USA. 2023.

36. *Phật Giáo và Đại Dịch Coronavirus Covid-19*. Thích Nữ Giới Hương. NXB Hương Sen. USA. 2023

37. *Phật Giáo – Tầm Nhìn Lịch Sử Và Thực Hành*. Hiệu đính: Thích Hạnh Chánh và Thích Nữ Giới Hương. Eastern Book Linkers: Delhi 7. 2023.

1.2. THE ENGLISH BOOKS

1. *Boddhisattva and Sunyata in the Early and Developed Buddhist Traditions,* Bhikṣuṇī Gioi Huong, Delhi-7: Eastern Book Linkers, 1st print 2004, 2nd reprint 2005 & Vietnam Buddhist University: 3rd reprint 2010.

2. *Rebirth Views in the Śūraṅgama Sūtra,* Dr. Bhikṣuṇī Giới Hương, Fifth Edition, Hồng Đức Publishing: Tủ Sách Bảo Anh Lạc. 2018.

3. *Commentary of Avalokiteśvara Bodhisattva,* Dr. Bhikṣuṇī Giới Hương, Fourth Edition, Hồng Đức Publishing: Tủ Sách Bảo Anh Lạc. 2018.

4. *The Key Words in Vajracchedikā Sūtra*, Thích Nữ Giới Hương,   Hồng Đức Publishing. 2020.

5. *Sārnātha-The Cradle of Buddhism in the Archeological View.* Hồng Đức Publishing. 2020.

6. *Take Refuge in the Three Gems and Keep the Five Precepts,* Thích Nữ Giới Hương, Hồng Đức Publishing. 2020.

7. *Cycle of Life*, Thích Nữ Giới Hương, Hồng Đức Publishing. 2020.

8. *Forty Years in the Dharma: A Life of Study and Service— Venerable Bhikṣuṇī Giới Hương*. Thích Nữ Viên Quang, TN Viên Nhuận, TN Viên Tiến, and TN Viên Khuông, Xpress Print Publishing, USA. 2020.

9. *Sharing the Dharma -Vietnamese Buddhist Nuns in the United States*, Thích Nữ Giới Hương, Hồng Đức Publishing. 2020.

10. *A Vietnamese Buddhist Nun and American Inmates.* 5th Edition. Bhikṣuṇī Thích Nữ Giới Hương. Hương Sen Press Publishing, USA. 2021.

11. *Daily Monastic Chanting,* Bhikṣuṇī Thích Nữ Giới Hương composed. Hương Sen Publisher. 2023.

12. *Weekly Buddhist Discourse Chanting,* vol 1, Bhikṣuṇī Thích Nữ Giới Hương composed. Hương Sen Publisher. 2023.

13. *Practice Meditation and Pure Land*, Bhikṣuṇī Thích Nữ Giới Hương composed. Hương Sen Publisher. 2023.

14. *The Ceremony for Peace*, Bhikṣuṇī Thích Nữ Giới Hương composed. Hương Sen Publisher. 2023.

15. *The Lunch Offering Ritual*, Bhikṣuṇī Thích Nữ Giới Hương composed. Hương Sen Publisher. 2023.

16. *The Ritual Offering Food to Hungry Ghosts*, Bhikṣuṇī Thích Nữ Giới Hương composed. Hương Sen Publisher. 2023.

17. *The Pureland Course of Amitabha Sutra*, Bhikṣuṇī Thích Nữ Giới Hương composed. Hương Sen Publisher. 2023.

18. *The Medicine Buddha Sutra*, Bhikṣuṇī Thích Nữ Giới Hương composed. Hương Sen Publisher. 2023.

19. *The New Year Ceremony*, Bhikṣuṇī Thích Nữ Giới Hương composed. Hương Sen Publisher. 2023.

20. *The Great Parinirvana Ceremony*, Bhikṣuṇī Thích Nữ Giới Hương composed. Hương Sen Publisher. 2023.

21. *The Buddha's Birthday Ceremony*, Bhikṣuṇī Thích Nữ Giới Hương composed. Hương Sen Publisher. 2023.

22. *The Ullambana Festival (Parents' Day)*, Bhikṣuṇī Thích Nữ Giới Hương composed. Hương Sen Publisher. 2023.

23. *The Marriage Ceremony*, Bhikṣuṇī Thích Nữ Giới Hương composed. Hương Sen Publisher. 2023.

24. *The Blessing Ceremony for The Deceased*, Bhikṣuṇī Thích Nữ Giới Hương composed. Hương Sen Publisher. 2023.

25. *The Ceremony Praising Ancestral Masters*, Bhikṣuṇī Thích Nữ Giới Hương composed. Hương Sen Publisher. 2023.

26. *The Enlightened Buddha Ceremony*, Bhikṣuṇī Thích Nữ Giới Hương composed. Hương Sen Publisher. 2023.

27. *The Uposatha Ceremony (Reciting Precepts)*, Bhikṣuṇī Thích Nữ Giới Hương composed. Hương Sen Publisher. 2023.

28. *Buddhism: A Historical And Practical Vision.* Edited by Ven.

Dr. Thich Hanh Chanh and Ven. Dr. Bhikṣuṇī TN Gioi Huong. Eastern Book Linkers: Delhi 7. 2023.

29. *Contribution of Buddhism For World Peace & Social Harmony.* Edited by Ven. Dr. Buddha Priya Mahathero and Ven. Dr. Bhikṣuṇī TN Gioi Huong. Tôn Giáo Publishing. 2023.

30. *Global Spread of Buddhism with Special Reference to Sri Lanka.* Buddhist Studies Seminar in Kandy University. Edited by Prof. Ven. Medagama Nandawansa and Dr. Bhikṣuṇī TN Gioi Huong. Tôn Giáo Publishing. 2023.

31. *Buddhism in Sri Lanka During The Period of 19ᵗʰ to 21st Centuries.* Buddhist Studies Seminar in Colombo. Edited by Prof. Ven. Medagama Nandawansa and Dr. Bhikṣuṇī TN Gioi Huong. Tôn Giáo Publishing. 2023.

1.3. THE BILINGUAL BOOKS (VIETNAMESE-ENGLISH)

1. *Bản Tin Hương Sen: Xuân, Phật Đản, Vu Lan (*Hương Sen Newsletter: Spring, Buddha Birthday and Vu Lan, annual/ Mỗi Năm). 2019 & 2020.

2. *Danh Ngôn Nuôi Dưỡng Nhân Cách - Good Sentences Nurture a Good Manner,* Thích Nữ Giới Hương sưu tầm, Hồng Đức Publishing. 2020.

3. *Văn Hóa Đặc Sắc của Nước Nhật Bản-Exploring the Unique Culture of Japan,* Thích Nữ Giới Hương. Hồng Đức Publishing. 2020.

4. *Sống An Lạc dù Đời không Đẹp như Mơ - Live Peacefully though Life is not Beautiful as a Dream*, Thích Nữ Giới Hương. Hồng Đức Publishing. 2020.

5. *Hãy Nói Lời Yêu Thương-Words of Love and Understanding,* Thích Nữ Giới Hương. Hồng Đức Publishing. 2020.

6. *Văn Hóa Cổ Kim qua Hành Hương Chiêm Bái -The Ancient-Present Culture in Pilgrim,* Thích Nữ Giới Hương. Hồng Đức

Publishing. 2020.

7. *Nghệ Thuật Biết Sống - Art of Living*. Thích Nữ Giới Hương, Hồng Đức Publishing. 2020.

1.4. THE TRANSLATED BOOKS

1. *Xá Lợi Của Đức Phật* (Relics of the Buddha), Tham Weng Yew, Thích Nữ Giới Hương chuyển ngữ, Delhi-7: Tủ Sách Bảo Anh Lạc, 2005. Delhi 2006: 2nd reprint. Tổng Hợp Tp HCM Publishing: the 3rd and 4th reprint in 2008 & 2016.

2. *Sen Nở Nơi Chốn Tử Tù* (Lotus in Prison), many authors, Thích Nữ Giới Hương translated from English into Vietnamese, Văn Hóa Sài gòn Publishing: Tủ Sách Bảo Anh Lạc, 2010. The 2nd, 3rd and 4th reprint in 2012, 2014 & 2016.

3. *Chùa Việt Nam Hải Ngoại* (Overseas Vietnamese Buddhist Temples), Võ Văn Tường & Từ Hiếu Côn, vol 2. Translated into English: Thích Nữ Giới Hương. Hương Quê Publishing. 2016.

4. *Việt Nam Danh Lam Cổ Tự* (The Famous Ancient Buddhist Temples in Vietnam), Võ Văn Tường. Translated into English: Thích Nữ Giới Hương. Phương Nam Publishing. 2016.

5. *Hương Sen, Thơ và Nhạc* – (Lotus Fragrance, Poem and Music), Nguyễn Hiền Đức. Translated into English: Thích Nữ Giới Hương. Hồng Đức Publishing. 2020.

6. *Phật Giáo-Một Bậc Đạo Sư, Nhiều Truyền Thống* (Buddhism: One Teacher – Many Traditions), Đức Đạt Lai Lạt Ma 14th & Ni Sư Thubten Chodren, Translated into Vietnamese: Ven. Dr. Thích Nữ Giới Hương, Prajna Upadesa Foundation Publshing. 2018.

7. *Cách Chuẩn Bị Chết và Giúp Người Sắp Chết-Quan Điểm Phật Giáo* (Preparing for Death and Helping the Dying – A Buddhist Perspective), Sangye Khadro, Translated into Vietnamese: Thích Nữ Giới Hương. Hồng Đức Publishing. 2020.

2. BUDDHIST MUSIC ALBUMS
from POEMS of THÍCH NỮ GIỚI HƯƠNG

1. Đào Xuân Lộng Ý Kinh (The Buddha's Teachings Reflected in Cherry Flowers), Poems: Thích Nữ Giới Hương. Music: Nam Hưng, Vol. 1. 2013.

2. *Niềm Tin Tam Bảo* (Trust in the Three Gems), Poems: Thích Nữ Giới Hương. Music: Hoàng Y Vũ and Hoàng Quang Huế, Vol. 2. 2013.

3. *Trăng Tròn Nghìn Năm Đón Chờ Ai* (Who Is the Full Moon Waiting for for Over a Thousand Years?). Poems: Thích Nữ Giới Hương. Music: Võ Tá Hân, Hoàng Y Vũ, Khánh Hải, Khánh Hoàng, Hoàng Kim Anh, Linh Phương và Nguyễn Tuấn, Vol. 3. 2013.

4. Ánh Trăng Phật Pháp (Moonlight of Dharma-Buddha). Poems: Thích Nữ Giới Hương. Music: Uy Thi Ca and Giác An, Vol. 4. 2013.

5. *Bình Minh Tỉnh Thức* (Awakened Mind at the Dawn) (*Piano Variations for Meditation*). Poems: Thích Nữ Giới Hương. Solo Pianist: Linh Phương, vol. 5. 2013.

6. *Tiếng Hát Già Lam* (Songs from the Temple). Poems: Thích Nữ Giới Hương. Music: Nam Hưng, vol. 6. 2015.

7. *Cảnh Đẹp Chùa Xưa* (The Magnificent, Ancient Buddhist Temple). Poem: Thích Nữ Giới Hương. Music: Võ Tá Hân, Nam Hưng, Hoàng Quang Huế, vol. 7. 2015.

8. Karaoke *Hoa Ưu Đàm Đã Nở* (An Udumbara Flower Is Blooming). Poem: Thích Nữ Giới Hương. Musician: Nam Hưng, Hương Sen Temple. 2015.

9. *Hương Sen Ca* (Hương Sen's Songs), Thơ: Thích Nữ Giới Hương. Nhạc: Nam Hưng, vol. 9, năm 2018.

10. *Về Chùa Vui Tu* (Happily Go to Temple for Spiritual Practices), Poem: Thích Nữ Giới Hương. Music: Nam Hưng and Nguyễn Hà. Volume 10. 2018.

11. *Gọi Nắng Xuân Về* (Call the Spring Sunlight), Poem: Thích Nữ
    Giới Hương. Music: Nam Hưng, Hương Sen Temple. Volume
    11. 2020.

12. Đệ tử Phật (The Buddha's Disciples). Poems: Thích Nữ Giới
    Hương. Music: Uy Thi Ca and Giác An, Album 12. 2023.

Please consult the **Bảo Anh Lạc Bookshelf** *at this website:*

*http://huongsentemple.com/index.php/en/about-us/b-o-anh-l-c-
bookshelf*

CONTRIBUTIONS OF BUDDHISM FOR WORLD PEACE
& SOCIAL HARMONY

Tác giả: Bảo Anh Lạc Bookshelf 78 - Thích Nữ Giới Hương

NHÀ XUẤT BẢN TÔN GIÁO

53 Tràng Thi – Hoàn Kiếm - Hà Nội

ĐT: (024)37822845

Email: nhaxuatbantongiao@gmail.com

Chịu trách nhiệm xuất bản

Giám đốc

ThS. Nguyễn Hữu Có

Chịu trách nhiệm nội dung

Tổng Biên tập

Lê Hồng Sơn

Biên tập: **Nguyễn Thị Thanh Thủy**

Trình bày: **Vũ Đình Trọng**

Sửa bản in: **Vũ Đình Trọng**

Số lượng in: 1.000 bản, Khổ: 15,24 x 22,86 cm

*In tại: Công ty TNHH Sản xuất Thương mại Dịch vụ In ấn Trâm Anh,
159/57 Bạch Đằng, phường 2, quận Tân Bình, thành phố Hồ Chí Minh.*

Số ĐKXB: 2090-2023/CXBIPH/12-94/TG

Mã ISBN: 978-604-61-9647-5

QĐXB: 471/QĐ-NXBTG ngày 20 tháng 9 năm 2023

In xong và nộp lưu chiểu quý III năm 2023